TOWARDS THE RESCUE
OF STERLING

TOWARDS
THE RESCUE
OF STERLING

R. G. HAWTREY

LONGMANS, GREEN AND CO
LONDON · NEW YORK · TORONTO

LONGMANS, GREEN AND CO LTD
6 & 7 CLIFFORD STREET LONDON W1
ALSO AT MELBOURNE AND CAPE TOWN

LONGMANS, GREEN AND CO INC
55 FIFTH AVENUE NEW YORK 3

LONGMANS, GREEN AND CO
215 VICTORIA STREET TORONTO 1

ORIENT LONGMANS LTD
BOMBAY CALCUTTA MADRAS

First published 1954

PRINTED IN GREAT BRITAIN
BY WESTERN PRINTING SERVICES LTD., BRISTOL

Preface

Is the pound sterling in need of rescue? There have been
crises in 1947, 1949 and 1951, but now the series seems to
have been broken; we have passed through two years without a crisis, and 1953 has been a year of relative calm.
Cannot matters be left to take their course?

Threatening symptoms are not wanting. And the study
which occupies the following pages discloses grave reasons
for mistrusting the apparent calm. We are often warned
against complacency, but a mere disavowal of complacency
is not enough; the portents are such that action is imperative—and *early* action.

A year ago in December 1952 the Commonwealth
Economic Conference discussed the conditions for the
restoration of sterling convertibility, and Mr. Butler,
addressing the Council of Ministers of the O.E.E.C. in
March 1953, specified among these conditions that progress
towards convertibility must depend on a 'good creditor
policy' on the part of the United States. This, he said, he
had made clear in Washington. And at the next meeting
(October 1953) he was reported as saying that the British
Government would not only wait until the Randall Com-
mission had reported, but would have to see what legislation
would follow.

It is not certain that much or anything can be expected
from changes in American policy, and in any case we cannot afford to wait. Time lost means a further deterioration
of the situation.

My object in writing, however, has not been solely to
urge warning of pending trouble. It has been still more to
indicate what form I believe remedial action ought to take.

In tracing the course of events since the war, I have made

full use of the statistical material relating to the National Income and the Balance of Payments, which emanates nowadays from the Government. Arguments built on statistics should be qualified by caution, and that much of this material is subject to wide margins of error I am well aware. But its value is none the less in illustrating the successive steps of my reasoning.

It is to the reasoning itself that I make my appeal. The statistics give it concrete form. That they do confirm it will, I hope, help to carry conviction.

The first half of the book, Chapters 1–3, surveys the events and measures of the years 1946–52. The rest is concerned with the problems and needs of the present and future.

My thesis can be summed up in a few sentences. The two-fold troubles of the present time, inflation and an adverse balance of payments, are both attributable to excessive spending. Exhortations to save and not to spend have become familiar to us. But saving means providing funds for capital outlay, and, for our present purpose, spending includes capital outlay itself, as well as consumption and Government expenditure. Excessive spending means spending in excess of income and therefore in excess of production, and in default of sufficient production, has to be met from traders' stocks of goods. It is the orders given for the replenishment of stocks that result, on the one hand, in the over-employment of industry, with inflationary effect; on the other, in additional imports.

The adverse balance of payments is caused not only by the additional imports, but by the over-employment of export industries, the diversion of their output to the home market, and the delays in delivery, which put producers at a disadvantage in export markets.

The excess spending is only possible if people have the *money* to spend, or facilities to procure it. The remedy is to be sought in financial and monetary measures.

The financial measures include an adequate tax revenue,

and Government loans subscribed from current savings, so that its spending is fully offset by a diminution of spending by the public.

The monetary measures include a credit policy which deters traders from resorting too freely to the holding of stocks of goods with borrowed money. The purchase of goods for the replenishment of stocks, 'active accumulation', is to be counted as 'spending'. Tight credit, by cutting down the supply of money for the active accumulation of stocks, immediately diminishes this form of excess spending, and at the same time restricts the stock of money available for further spending.

Can money, a mere medium, do so much? Long experience has shown that it can. A change in credit conditions permeates all economic life. It is like a change of atmosphere, such as that from an east wind to a west. The summer east wind brings a heat wave, and veils the distance in a thin arid haze. A little cloud, like a man's hand, heralds the transformation to clear, fresh, limpid air and white billowing clouds.

R. G. HAWTREY

January 1954

CONTENTS

Chapter   *page*

I. THE CONVERTIBILITY CRISIS OF 1947
   Impoverishment   1
   The Balance of Payments and the Con-
     vertibility Crisis   5
   Exchange Control and the Special Accounts   7
   Inflation and Excess Spending   13
   Redundant Money and Controls   15
   Abandonment of American Price Control   19
   The Demand for Dollars in 1947   21
   Import Restrictions and the Sterling Area   25

II. THE DEVALUATION OF 1949
   The Dollar Balance, 1947–9   28
   The Devaluation of 1949   30
   Inflation and Deflation in the United States,
     1946–9   36
   Import Restrictions and Consumption   38
   Redundant Money and Monetary Policy   40
   The International Monetary Fund   43
   Prices after Devaluation   45

III. ARMAMENTS AND NATIONAL FINANCE
   Korea and Prices of Materials   48
   Armaments and Taxation   50
   Capital Formation and Resources   54
   The Change of Government and Monetary
     Policy   59
   The Budget Position   60
   Prices and Profits   62
   Devaluation and Import Prices   66

ix

Chapter   *page*

    Devaluation and Redundant Money   67
    British and American Productivity   69
    Exporting Power   71

IV. CREDIT POLICY
    The English Credit System   73
    Influence of Bank Rate on Borrowing   75
    The Rise of Bank Rate in 1952   79
    The Deficit   80
    A Flexible Bank Rate   82
    Spending and Capital Formation   83
    Active Accumulation   85
    The Acceptable Level of Stocks   89

V. CAPITAL OUTLAY AND EXTERNAL INVESTMENT
    External Investment   93
    The Dollar Balance   96
    Investment in the Sterling Area   99
    Credit Policy and Capital Outlay   102
    Government Securities and the Investment
      Market   105
    Overseas Sterling Balances   108

VI. PROSPECTS AND POLICIES
    Inflation and the Wage Level   111
    An Up-Valuation of the Pound   114
    Wages and Export Costs   118
    The Near Future   120
    Bank Rate and Government Securities   124
    Full Employment and Over-Employment   125
    A Monetary Standard   130
    Welfare, Capital and Defence   136
    Austerity   139

INDEX   145

Chapter One

THE CONVERTIBILITY CRISIS OF 1947

IMPOVERISHMENT

GREAT BRITAIN was gravely impoverished by the Second World War, and impoverishment has been found to mean weakness, which has been felt in a deterioration of military power and of political influence.

In so far as the strain of the war effort was met by reducing consumption and by increasing productive activity through additional manpower, fuller employment and longer hours of work, the cost was currently met, and no accumulated loss emerged at the end. And the greater part of the cost, perhaps two-thirds, was covered in this way. But there was a residue met out of the country's accumulated wealth, and it is of this loss of accumulated wealth that impoverishment is the outcome.

Particulars of the loss, so far as it could be estimated at the end of the war, were set out in the Statistical Material presented during the Washington negotiations (Cmd. 6707 of December 1945). The outstanding item was the 'External Disinvestment' exceeding £4,000 million, and including £1,118 million from realisation of capital assets, £303 million from overseas loans and £2,576 million from a net increase in floating indebtedness in the form of sterling balances held abroad. To this total had soon to be added the American and Canadian loans amounting (before the devaluation of 1949) to some £1,400 million. From the greatest of creditor nations Great Britain had become the greatest of debtors.

Two centuries of lucrative trade, industry and finance had

1

put the country in a position to support a population far in excess of the numbers which the natural products of the land they occupied could provide for. Their economic life was crucially dependent on the continuance of imported supplies of food and materials, and these supplies were paid for only in part by exports of goods, but also by the interest and profits on external investments, by the mercantile and financial profits of international trade, and by the earnings of shipping.

British shipping was disastrously diminished by wartime losses, and the scope for earning mercantile profits was contracted by the dislocation of international trade, by shackling controls, and by the intervention of Governments to perform functions which would ordinarily fall to traders.

The immediate preoccupation of the British authorities in 1945 was the need to expand exports to fill the gap in the means of payment for essential imports. The export trade had been in any case curtailed during the war: some markets were cut off by enemy occupation; others were reduced by war conditions to a state of siege; shipping facilities were heavily reduced by sinkings and by wartime priorities. And what was left of British exporting power was ruthlessly sacrificed by the transfer of the productive resources of industry to the direct supply of the war effort.

The British Government estimated (Cmd. 6707, para. 12) that 'the full restoration of a reliable equilibrium, which can persist without measures of restriction or the other defensive mechanisms of the type with which it is hoped to dispense, may require a volume of exports nearer 75 per cent. than 50 per cent. in excess of the pre-war level'.

In 1944 the volume of exports was no more than 31 per cent. of what it had been in 1938. To raise it from 31 to 150 or 175 was a formidable task.

An expansion of exports cannot be automatically ensured by an increase of production beyond home needs. The exports must find markets, and must be of a kind to suit these markets. But in the circumstances of 1945 and several succeeding years all the markets of the world had been kept short of supplies of manufactured goods, and there was no difficulty in finding buyers. So long as that was so, the problem of exports could be regarded as no more than a problem of production, or rather of production in excess of home needs. Home needs had been subjected during the war to a policy of austerity enforced by rationing and other controls. The war ended, the policy of austerity was re-inforced by an export drive, in pursuance of which manu-facturers were persuaded or compelled to reserve a certain proportion of their output for export. Without obtaining formal compulsory powers, the Government could put pressure on the manufacturers through their control of the importation and allocation of materials.

Evidently a revival of production was the urgent need. Demobilisation and the release of labour from the war industries provided manpower. To set the hands to work, the material means of production were needed, equipment and materials.

And here we turn to another part of the loss of accumu-lated wealth, the deterioration of capital equipment and property at home. Destruction by enemy action was, of course, a heavy item. War damage compensation, even now hardly complete, has reached £2,000 million. That total is swollen by the post-war rise of costs and prices. But even reckoned at contemporary values, it must have exceeded £1,000 million.

But the deterioration through insufficiency of upkeep and renewals was even more serious. The Washington White Paper (Cmd. 6707, p. 13) put Disinvestment within the United Kingdom in the five years 1940–4 at £885 million. But that calculation was based on data which were sub-sequently revised. The National Income White Paper issued in April 1947 (Cmd. 7099) gave, under the head, Net Capital Formation at Home, in the five years, a minus quantity totalling £1,531 million.

And even that was an under-statement. It was arrived

at by deducting the estimated capital formation year by year from the assumed provision for depreciation. But the depreciation allowance was to start with admittedly incomplete, and no provision was made for increased allowances as costs rose. For a measure of the rise of costs we may take the index of weekly wages, which rose from 100 in September 1939 to 150 in 1945. The following table shows the equivalent at pre-war costs (in £ millions) of the capital formation in each year:

TABLE I

			Actual Outlay	Wage Index	Pre-war Equivalent
1940	...	...	268	112·2	239
1941	...	...	176	122·2	144
1942	...	...	202	131·0	154
1943	...	...	198	136·7	145
1944	...	...	97	143·7	68

The total equivalent for the five years adds up to £750 million or an average of £150 million a year. The capital formation in 1938 was reckoned at £770 million, of which depreciation accounted for £450 million, leaving net accumulation of £320 million.

Therefore, capital formation in the years 1940–4 fell short of depreciation by £300 million a year in terms of pre-war costs. In 1946 the wage index rose to 161·5, so that the arrears of capital outlay, reckoned at the costs then prevailing, would be nearly £2,500 million.

This calculation, however, makes some rather unrealistic assumptions. The depreciation allowance does not represent renewals actually falling due; it is an accounting device, indicating the amount that ought to be accumulated towards future renewals. In a growing community depreciation allowances would exceed the current expenditure on renewals. On the other hand, depreciation allowances usually aim at providing replacement of plant only when it wears out; they make little or no provision for earlier obsolescence, and a part of what is nominally classed as payment to reserve is rather additional depreciation provided against obsolescence than true saving.

Moreover a growing community needs capital extensions to provide for the employment of the additional population. An estimate of the arrears accumulated during the war should include these necessary extensions as well as the necessary renewals that were postponed.

Thus the figure of £2,500 million arrived at above may well be an under-statement rather than an over-statement of the capital arrears to be dealt with in the post-war years.

Capital formation for the purposes of the annual National Income Return includes additions to stocks of goods and other forms of working capital. A part of the £2,500 million is accounted for by reductions of stocks. Stocks of many kinds of goods had been so heavily drawn on during the war as to be reduced below the workable minimum. Shop shortages were playing a substantial part in restricting consumption.

THE BALANCE OF PAYMENTS AND THE CONVERTIBILITY CRISIS

The restoration of the export trade depended on the restoration of production, and the restoration of production depended on the restoration of the capital equipment of industry. War damage and arrears of capital outlay had to be made good. But where were the requisite resources to come from? Even if the country's productive power had been in full working trim, an additional capital outlay running to several thousands of millions would have taken a number of years. And since the cessation of Lend–Lease in September 1945, the immediate problem had been the procurement of essential imports.

That was the primary purpose of the American and Canadian loans. In the year 1946 imports were drastically restricted, and amounted to only 68·3 per cent. of their pre-war volume. But there was still an adverse balance of £298 million, towards meeting which the American and Canadian loans provided £279 million.

With a given level of consumption an adverse balance of payments is an additional capital resource. That is so, even though the actual goods imported are for consumption, for, if consumption is not thereby increased, productive power is set free for capital outlay. The adverse balance is essentially an excess of spending over income—spending in a wide sense, to include capital outlay as well as consumption.

In 1946 the British budget was still heavily in deficit. The excess of expenditure and revenue in the calendar year was £906 million. Much of this was for disbursements, such as war gratuities, war damage compensation and refunds of excess profits tax, which are reckoned as Transfers to Capital Account.[1] And the excess does not count as revenue the large sums (£92 million at home and £164 million abroad) received from sales of surplus war stores and from war settlements, etc., abroad. After making these adjustments there still remained a big deduction from the capital resources available from current savings, and the net amount remaining, £584 million (see below, p. 57), cannot have provided much margin above necessary depreciation. The capital outlay of the year was £900 million, of which the rest was mainly provided from the American and Canadian loans.

In 1947 full use began to be made of the resources provided by the loans, and imports were admitted somewhat more freely. Great Britain had an adverse balance on current account with the Dollar Area of £510 million. And the overseas Sterling Area, where arrears of expenditure were not less pressing, had an adverse dollar balance of £306 million. The American and Canadian loans were drawn on to a total amount of £812 million, a sum nearly sufficient

---

[1] They are rightly counted as purely capital items, for, though they may be spent partly on consumption, they are excluded from income in the calculation of personal saving. In that calculation (Table 2 of the National Income Return) the whole of consumption expenditure is deducted from such receipts as are reckoned as income.

to cover the adverse balances with the Dollar Area. Yet the British gold and dollar reserves were drawn on to the amount of £152 million.

It was at this time that the convertibility of sterling in pursuance of the Loan Agreement of 6th December 1945 came into effect. Holders of sterling hastened to take advantage of the facilities that became available to them to convert it into dollars, and there resulted net payments of dollars from the Sterling Area to non-dollar countries amounting (for the whole year) to £198 million ($798 million).

The reserve position at the time was weak. The American loan of $3,750 million had been a disappointment: the amount fell substantially short of what the Government and Keynes himself had thought requisite and had hoped for. The hard winter of 1946–7 and the resulting fuel and transport crisis had caused a serious interruption of the process of industrial recovery and British exports in the first two quarters of 1947 fell some ten per cent. below the volume attained at the end of 1946. American wages and prices were rising, so that the value of the dollars obtained from the loan in terms of goods was falling. When convertibility came into operation on the 15th July 1947, more than half the loan had already been used up, and the remainder was being rapidly drawn on. On the 20th August it became necessary to obtain the consent of the American Government to the suspension of convertibility after only six weeks' trial.

The breakdown had an essentially monetary character. The convertibility that had to be suspended was not of money into goods, or of goods into money, but of money into money.

EXCHANGE CONTROL AND THE SPECIAL ACCOUNTS

To understand the convertibility crisis of 1947, and indeed the subsequent phases of the convertibility question, it is necessary to have regard to the nature and purpose of the wartime controls applied to the foreign exchanges. When exchange control was imposed at the outbreak of war in September 1939, the immediate aim was to gather into the Government's control the foreign exchange in or coming into private hands. Everyone was required under penalty to sell to the Government (through the banks) any gold or 'hard currency' he might possess or receive,[1] hard currency being defined to include American dollars and certain other money units deemed eligible for use as the means of payment in international markets. The holder of hard currency who retained it was withholding it from the nation's use in procuring oversea supplies for the war effort.

The Government, so long as it undertook to supply foreign money (at official rates of exchange) for any legitimate purpose, could reasonably require the sale to it (at the same rates) of any foreign money not needed for any legitimate purpose. Legitimate purposes included payment for permitted imports. Imports of goods, along with ancillary expenses such as shipping freights, were restricted by a system of licensing, and, where the purpose of an external payment could thus be made subject to control, payment could be allowed automatically. But in other cases, where the payment itself had to be made the occasion of control, it was for the Exchange Control authorities to determine whether the purpose of any transaction was such as public policy could permit. The general principle was to prohibit capital movements, whether external investment or the transfer of balances abroad.

It was not enough to control transactions in foreign money. Payments in sterling to or from abroad had the same effect on the foreign exchange position as payments in foreign money. Every country must ultimately recover payment for its exports in its own money, but, in virtue of the position of sterling as an international currency, it was

---

[1] Needless to say, possession of a currency included possession of a bank balance payable in the currency.

very usual for the immediate settlement for British imports as well as for British exports to be in sterling.

British exports were of course ultimately the means of earning foreign exchange, and it was essential for the efficient administration of the Exchange Control to keep track of the proceeds of exports. Exporters could not be required to surrender the proceeds in foreign money without upsetting the whole system of payment both ways in sterling.

An alternative was found in dealing with the proceeds of imports instead of the proceeds of exports. When imports were paid for in sterling, the foreign seller would of course eventually need the equivalent in the money of his own country, in which his costs had been incurred, and in which he would want his own income to be reckoned. The sterling received by him would, therefore, be a potential demand upon the foreign exchange market for this foreign money. If a British exporter could show that he had received payment in sterling thus potentially equivalent to foreign money, he would be supporting the foreign exchange position of the country as effectively as if he had handed over the same amount in foreign money. The claims of foreign exporters for their own money would be met by their own Governments, and the British monetary reserves would be relieved from them. And so long as British exporters were paid in sterling and received no foreign money, the evasion of exchange control by accumulating the proceeds of exports in foreign money or foreign assets would be guarded against.

In applying this arrangement, the distinction between hard and soft currencies had to be preserved. An exporter who sold his goods to a hard-currency country would not discharge his obligations adequately by accepting sterling which would be destined to be converted into a soft currency. And it was not enough simply to set up a broad classification of money units once for all into hard and soft. There were degrees of hardness and softness, and the classification was liable to fluctuate according to the varying exigencies of policy. It was, therefore, decided to apply the system to each country or currency area separately. Sterling received by inhabitants of any country or currency area for exports to Great Britain was to be paid into 'special accounts', out of which payment was to be made for its imports from Great Britain. The British exporter escaped the obligation to surrender foreign currency when he could show that he had been paid from a special account of the importing country. Once the money was in British hands, the potential demand for foreign money was extinguished, for the British holder could not buy foreign exchange with it, or pay it to the credit of a foreign account, without the permission of the Exchange Control.

Money could be freely transferred from a special account to another special account of the same country, for the transfer left the potential demand for foreign exchange unaltered. But transfer to a special account of another country was not allowed. It might transform a potential soft currency liability into a potential hard currency liability.

During the war the special account system was generally adopted, but there were two large exceptions.

The Sterling Area (composed of the British Empire, except Canada, together with a few foreign countries) formed a group within which free movements of money were allowed, so that for the purposes of exchange control it was a unit. All the countries composing the Sterling Area adopted substantially the same code of exchange control, and they co-ordinated their import restrictions. For the purposes, therefore, of the special account system, British imports and exports must be taken to mean the imports and exports of the Sterling Area.

Another group was formed by the United States and certain countries of Latin America, whose monetary arrangements were so closely associated with those of the United States that they could be treated together as a single Dollar Area. All sterling acquired by the Dollar Area in payment for exports to the Sterling Area was freely convertible into dollars.

It was Article 8 (ii) of the Loan Agreement of 6th December 1945 that required an extended convertibility of sterling. Under that Article the Governments of the United States and the United Kingdom agreed that 'not later than one year after the effective date of this Agreement . . . they will impose no restrictions on payments and transfers for current transactions'. The undertaking did not apply to sterling accruing before the critical date, and thereafter it applied only to the use of sterling in 'current transactions'.

The British exchange control was in principle directed exclusively to preventing *capital* transactions, and to leaving current transactions free. Imports into Great Britain and into the other partners in the Sterling Area were restricted by prohibitions subject to licensing, but these restrictions were on the movement of goods, not on payment. Payment for permitted imports was unrestricted.

The restrictions on payments, against which the Anglo-American Loan Agreement was directed, were those arising out of the Special Account system. They had been imposed as a device for preventing evasion of the control of capital transactions, but none the less did restrict payments for current transactions. If they were abandoned, sterling accruing to any country from exports to the Sterling Area could no longer be segregated in a special account from which it could be withdrawn only to pay for the country's own imports from the Sterling Area, but could be used to pay for imports from the Sterling Area into any other country. Sterling earned by a soft-currency country could, therefore, be transferred to a hard-currency country, and used, in place of hard currency, to pay for the latter's imports from the Sterling Area. The obligation placed on British exporters to account for their sales to hard-currency countries would be deprived of effect, for, if they sold for sterling, the sterling proceeds would no longer be the equivalent of hard currency.

This obligation had been imposed at an early stage of the war as a device for preventing evasion of the general obligation placed on everyone in the Sterling Area to sell hard currencies or their equivalent to the Government. The general obligation was still in operation. But was there any good reason for continuing it? The concentration of foreign exchange in the hands of the Government had been warranted by the imperative need to provide the maximum possible means of drawing on external resources for the war effort. The return to peace conditions brought different urgencies. The dominant demands of reconstruction and re-equipment forbade the diversion of capital resources into external investment. But self-interest would lead the owners of equipment and property to concentrate on its preservation, so that in the immediate post-war circumstances investment abroad was not likely to be a serious competitor with them for the resources of the capital market. For some lines of reconstruction, especially housing, the Government assumed responsibility, and raised the capital resources on its own account. And controls were retained, especially through the allocation of materials, the licensing of construction, and the restriction of capital issues, whereby capital projects and enterprises could be subjected to considerations of public policy.

In the regulation of capital enterprise, however, the exchange control played only a very minor part. It placed no impediment in the way of oversea investment in the Sterling Area, and, owing to political conditions, there was little inducement to invest outside it.

Why then could not exchange control be dispensed with? Why did convertibility break down?

The breakdown was, as stated above, a monetary crisis. The war had inflicted on the country not only impoverishment but monetary weakness.

INFLATION AND EXCESS SPENDING

The experience of two great wars has made the process of monetary inflation under the pressure of war finance only too familiar to the world. A Government which cannot raise sufficient revenue to pay for its war effort has recourse to borrowing. So long as what it borrows is provided from the lenders' current savings out of income, the Government can legitimately spend what the lenders thus refrain from spending. But when the Government cannot meet its expenditure from revenue and from legitimate borrowing, it borrows from the banks, and the banks have the dangerous power to *create* money by lending. When a bank buys a Treasury bill from the Government, two debts are created: the bill is a debt from the Government to the bank, while the debt from the bank to the Government, whether in the form of a deposit or of bank notes, can be used as a means of payment—money.

The Government thereby obtains the power of spending, while neither the bank nor anyone else is abstaining from spending. And, when the Government spends, it transfers the money to people in whose hands it is income ready for spending again.

So long as the productive power of the country is underemployed, the increased spending elicits increased production, but when production reaches capacity, the swollen demand forces up prices. It is the rise of prices that is popularly identified with inflation. But underlying the rise of prices, and preceding it, is the excess spending. Excess spending here means spending (whether on consumption or on capital enterprise) in excess of income.

If income is so defined as to be equal to production, spending in excess of income is spending in excess of production, and spending in excess of production must be met either from stocks of goods or from imports. The kinds of goods which traders hold in stock are nearly the same as the kinds of goods which are exported and imported. Imports may, therefore, be regarded as a supply for replenishing stocks. There may, of course, be imported goods which have been ordered by those who intend to use them, and which, therefore, are not destined to be held for sale in a trader's stock. But such direct orders, whether from foreign or home sources, if they are of goods that are ordinarily held in stock, take the place of sales from stock.

In principle, therefore, we may say that excess spending is met from stocks, and it is the replenishment of stocks that is supplied from imports.

Nor is our definition of income as being equal to production essential to this conclusion. The definition, though sound in itself and convenient for the purposes of economic theory, does not correspond very closely to the generally accepted idea of income. It excludes all 'transfer incomes', that is to say, those which are not paid in consideration of any current productive activity. The exclusion of voluntary allowances, such as those from parents to children, and of philanthropic donations and benefits, is natural enough. The exclusion of pensions, annuities and insurance benefits is not to be passed quite so readily. And the exclusion of interest on the national debt is an actual paradox.

But a definition of income to include some or all kinds of transfer incomes would not materially modify the calculation of excess spending. For the payment of the transfer incomes has then to be reckoned as part of the spending of the taxpayers, philanthropists, parents and others who provide them: they appear both as income and as expenditure, and do not alter the difference which is the excess spending.

During the war the British Government sought to avert the threat of inflation by controls. By restricting supplies for civilian consumption and use, and controlling prices, it was possible to limit civilian spending. Supplies were limited partly by imposing priority of war demands on all producers, partly by restricting imports. Rationing, where applicable, prevented any demand in excess of available supplies. Price controls limited the money value of the supplies people could procure. In short, civilian expenditure was limited to the value of the supplies available at officially-fixed prices. Any excess of incomes over the expenditure thus limited became savings available for the Government's wartime expenditure. Much of the excess was actually placed in Government securities; the rest swelled the total of bank deposits, against which Treasury bills, Treasury deposit receipts, or other Government securities were held by the banks.

The Government's own excess expenditure continued, but the controls prevented it from generating further excess expenditure on the part of individuals. The controls, however, were not quite rigorously effective. There was no control over wages, and though the price control, combined with subsidies, kept down the cost of living, there was an acute shortage of manpower, over-employment and an insistent demand for labour, which pushed up wages. By the end of the war the index of weekly wages showed an increase of 50 per cent. since 1938, and official prices had to be adjusted to costs, of which wages were the principal constituents.

The increase of 50 per cent. was in reality very moderate. The stock of money (bank deposits *plus* currency) had more than doubled. The trade union leaders had co-operated with the Government in keeping demands for higher wages in check. And the Government exercised considerable powers of control over the use of manpower, by which the edge could be taken off the demand for labour.

REDUNDANT MONEY AND CONTROLS

The pressure of the war effort on public finance lasted for some time after the war had come to an end. In the calendar year 1946, when Government expenditure exceeded revenue by £906 million, the deficit continued to be largely financed by the banks, and by the end of 1946 net bank deposits had reached £5,330 million, in comparison with £2,192 million at the end of 1938. Currency in the hands of the public had risen from £448 million to £1,356 million, so that the supply of money had increased by more than 150 per cent.[1]

In the same period the wage level had risen by only 61·5 per cent. There was, it is true, full employment, and the national income had risen by 73 per cent. On the other hand, a state of depression and unemployment, such as prevailed in the year of comparison, 1938, is always accompanied by a stagnation of money, so that the ratio of the supply of money to the flow of money is abnormally high.[2]

Had the supply of money (bank deposits *plus* currency) increased in the same proportion as the national income it would have amounted in 1946 to no more than £4,570 million. The actual supply was £6,686 million. If allowance be made for the state of stagnation prevailing in 1938, the amount of redundant money must have been much above £2,000 million.

Moreover this calculation takes account only of loose money or ready cash. Along with enlarged cash balances, people held very large sums in the form of Government securities, all readily marketable, and many of short maturity. A great part of the money they had been compelled to save during the war for want of opportunities of spending, they had invested in this way. Business concerns which had postponed capital outlay on renewals, improvements and extensions, or had let maintenance fall into arrears, or had failed to replenish stocks of goods, held the monetary equivalent of the expenditure they had postponed either in cash or in Government securities. And consumers who had had to postpone expenditure on the upkeep of property and on the replenishment of their personal possessions and household articles had done likewise.

Thus the people who held accumulations of money, and of securities that could be readily turned into money, were, for the most part, precisely those in whom the urge to spend

[1] This calculation excludes the Scottish and Northern Irish bank deposits and bank notes, but the result would not be materially affected thereby.

[2] In the years of depression from 1929 to 1938 the supply of money had increased by nearly 30 per cent. while the national income was little if at all higher in 1938 than in 1929.

was strongest. The mere urge to spend, if unsupported by the possession of money or of the means of raising money, is sterile. And the possession of money, if not accompanied by any desire to spend, fails to engender demand. The combination in 1946 of redundant money with an urgent need to make up arrears of spending was a highly combustible mixture, the imminent menace of an inordinate potential demand.

Against this threat of inflation the Government relied on the continuance of wartime controls. Rationing, so far as it extended, restricted demand. It was not confined to food, but was applied to clothing through the points system, and to some other commodities. Capital expenditure also was subjected to licensing and other forms of restriction.

The field covered by these devices for restricting demand at its source, though extensive, was limited. Outside its boundaries the full force of the swollen demand impinged upon the productive resources of the country. Indeed, just because demand was controlled in some directions, it was all the greater where it was free.

The controls were not exclusively directed to counteracting inflation. A concurrent aim, perhaps the primary aim, was to promote exports. The measures of austerity were designed to make productive power available for exports by restricting the home demand for exportable goods. While the rationing of food restricted the demand for imports, the rationing of clothing and furniture set free an exportable surplus.

Where rationing was not applied, the effect of the export drive was to reduce supplies at home without reducing demand. The Government's control of the import of materials, through licensing and its own bulk-purchasing, was used to require manufacturers, as a condition of receiving materials, to export a prescribed proportion of their output. Home-produced materials, such as coal and steel, were likewise allocated on conditions.

The natural result of a shortage of supplies in face of an

C

excess of money would be a rise of prices—a rise which would persist till the purchasing power of a unit of money was so reduced that the supply of money was no longer excessive. Or, in other words, the rise of prices would eventually absorb the excess of demand.

It is with this rise of prices that the dangers of inflation are popularly associated. For when the rise is in progress, there results a distrust of money, which manifests itself in a desire to part with money in exchange for goods, a desire to hold goods, which retain their value, in preference to money, which is losing its value. Distrust of money sets up a vicious circle. The more people seek to get rid of their money, the more rapidly prices rise, and the greater does the distrust become. Distrust, in fact, alters the relation between the stock of money and the flow of money. The existence of redundant money starts an expansion of the flow of money in the form of additional spending; there follow a rise of prices, a distrust of money and a further expansion of the flow of money; and eventually the flow of money, through income and outlay, will have been enlarged by the rise in the price level far more than in proportion to the original excess supply of money.

Undoubtedly, fear of this development was prominent among the motives both for adopting price control in Great Britain during the war, and for prolonging price control when the war was over. And the policy of price control was so far successful that the rise of prices immediately after the war was kept within moderate limits. The wholesale index (100 in 1938) rose from 167·9 in June 1945 to 171·0 in June 1946, or less than 2 per cent. There was no panic distrust of the currency.

But that did not mean that the effects of inflation were entirely counteracted. The urge to spend was none the less there; in fact, it was intensified by the control of prices. The controls interposed no impediment in the way of people with money in hand ordering whatever goods they wanted. Producers found themselves overwhelmed with orders beyond what they could execute in any reasonable time, and deprived of their normal defence, a rise of prices.

Had imports been free of control, the demand which producers at home could not satisfy would have been diverted abroad. But the quantitative restriction of imports was an essential part of the policy of austerity. The volume of imports was actually kept at a lower level than during the war. In 1946 it was only 68·3 per cent. of what it had been in 1938, in comparison with 80 per cent. in 1944.

Exchange control may be regarded as supplementing the restriction of imports of material products with a restriction of invisible imports. Invisible imports include such items as travellers' expenditure abroad, but the most important category is external investment, in the broad sense of the accumulation of resources abroad. It was the prevention of external investment that had been the ground for restricting the convertibility of sterling in the manner described above.

ABANDONMENT OF AMERICAN PRICE CONTROL

In July 1947, when the pledge given to the United States to make sterling convertible took effect, there seemed to be no reason to fear a panic flight from sterling into foreign investment. Why, then, did convertibility break down?

In the immediate post-war period Great Britain and the United States were the two principal sources of supply of manufactured products to the world. Up to 1946 the United States followed much the same policy of price control as Great Britain. But the United States had no need of an export drive or of austerity, being far less dependent on imported food and materials, and having big exportable surpluses of certain kinds of both.

Price control had the same effects in the United States as in Great Britain. Traders were prevented from defending their stocks by raising prices, and gave all the more orders to manufacturers to replenish them. The value of stocks ('inventories') had only risen from $28,772 million at the end of 1941 to $30,571 million at the end of 1945. Prices meanwhile had risen, notwithstanding control, from an index of 87·3 in 1941 to 105·8 in 1945, and monthly sales from $16,412 million in 1941 to $24,181 million in 1945. There had evidently been a substantial decrease in the volume of stocks, while a state of full employment was reflected in an increase in the volume of sales.

In June 1946 the United States started to abandon price controls, and the process of suppressing them was practically completed by the end of the year. The supply of money had become excessive during the war, though not quite so conspicuously so as in Great Britain. In 1946 the national income was $180,300 million, and the supply of money (adjusted deposits *plus* currency) was $164,004, or 91 per cent. of a year's income. The proportion had at one time been higher in the years of depression; it reached 107·5 in 1932 and was still as high as 95·2 in 1934. But this was a time of extreme shrinkage of the national income and stagnation of cash balances. In 1941, the year before the United States entered the war, the supply of money was 73·5 per cent. of a year's income. (In 1929 it was as low as 62·4 per cent.)

If 73·5 per cent. be taken as normal, the supply of money corresponding to an income of $180,300 million a year would be $132,520 million and according to that calculation money to the amount of some $30,000 million was redundant.[1]

Nothing was done to counteract the expansion which the abandonment of price control released. The short-term rate of interest remained extremely low. And 'the sound principle of Government price support of bonds which the people have bought as an expression of their faith in the Government's financial security,'[2] meant in effect that Government bonds were readily realisable without loss, and

---

[1] The experience of subsequent years suggests that 73·5 per cent. may be above the normal proportion, for the proportion has fallen to 67 per cent. in 1951 and 66·9 per cent. in 1952.

[2] *The Economic Report of the President,* January 1948, p. 10. The Federal Reserve Banks intervened in the market by purchases to keep up the price of the bonds.

to the holders were the equivalent of money. Manufacturers and traders who had put their unspent accumulations of depreciation funds and undistributed profits in Government securities found no financial impediment in the way of drawing upon them to spend.

Even before the abandonment of price control there had been a noticeable acceleration of the rise of prices, and the wholesale index (100 in 1926) reached 112·9 in June 1946. By August 1948 it had risen to 169·5, a rise of 50 per cent. (or of 60 per cent. since 1945). Freedom to raise prices enabled traders to accumulate stocks. The rise in the value of stocks from $30,571 million at the end of 1945 to $56,756 million at the end of 1948 was much more than in proportion to prices. Sales had risen from $24,181 million a month in 1945 to $37,003 million in 1948. Stocks had thus been increased from 5·47 weeks' sales to 6·65 weeks'—a clear sign that the state of over-employment caused by price control had ceased or at any rate had been relieved. American manufacturers were no longer overburdened with orders. In contrast with British manufacturers who, when offered orders, could only promise delivery of goods after long delay, stretching in some cases not merely to months but to years, the Americans could ensure relatively prompt delivery.

THE DEMAND FOR DOLLARS IN 1947

In July 1947, when the convertibility of sterling took effect, this process had already gone far enough to give American exporters a decisive advantage over British. If markets were favourable to both, that was because the needs to be met in the importing countries were urgent. The convertibility of sterling meant that any soft-currency country which acquired sterling through its exports to the Sterling Area was no longer to find the money tied up for payment for its imports from the Sterling Area; it could use the sterling acquired to pay for imports from the United States or other hard-currency countries. A British exporter to a hard-currency country would accept in payment the sterling proceeds of exports from a soft-currency country to the Sterling Area. Therefore, traders in the hard-currency country, who had to pay for imports from the Sterling Area, would be willing to pay dollars for sterling transferred from the soft-currency country. The soft-currency countries would be able to intercept the dollar proceeds of exports from the Sterling Area to the Dollar Area.

Convertibility only applied to 'current transactions'. Sterling which had accrued before the 15th July 1947 was expressly excepted from Article 8 (ii) of the Agreement. Therefore the huge wartime accumulations of externally held sterling balances were excluded from its operation—an apparently important safeguard.

But all the current receipts in sterling of countries outside the Dollar Area from the Sterling Area became convertible. Exports from such countries to Great Britain amounted in 1947 to £500 million, and to that must be added their exports to the rest of the Sterling Area, and the gross proceeds of their invisible exports to the whole Sterling Area, all of which became convertible into dollars.

A soft-currency country, it may be said, could not afford to turn all its currently accruing sterling into dollars; it must retain enough to pay for its current imports from the Sterling Area. Any sterling accruing before the 15th July 1947 remained subject to restriction. But restriction did not prevent it from being used to pay for imports from the Sterling Area. Some of the wartime accumulations of externally held sterling had been the subject of agreements limiting the amount that could be immediately used, but some were still unrestricted. And some countries had accumulated additional sterling balances since the end of the war. Any country could use its sterling freely to pay for its imports from the Sterling Area unless precluded by a specific agreement.

The sterling balances held in foreign countries, other than

the Dollar Area and the Sterling Area, at the end of 1946 amounted to £1,268 million.

The special accounts system was embodied in a series of separate agreements with the countries concerned, and convertibility necessitated revision of each of these agreements. A beginning had been made with the process of revision before the end of 1946, and convertibility came partially into operation before the stipulated date in July 1947 as the agreements came one after another under revision. When the 15th July arrived, there were still several of these agreements under negotiation and the American Government consented to convertibility being postponed in these cases till September. But even so the impact of convertibility appeared to be more than the resources of the Sterling Area could stand.

Of the $3,750 million of the American loan $2,050 million had been drawn in the twelve months ended 30th June 1947, and of the Canadian credit $676 million had been drawn by that date. In the ensuing quarter there were drawn further sums of $1,300 million and $150 million respectively, leaving only $400 million still available from the American loan and $333 million from the Canadian.[1]

Undoubtedly the rapid depletion of the loan resources was due principally to the urgent needs both of Great Britain and of the rest of the Sterling Area. The needs were greater and the wealth-value of loans was less than had been expected. But while it was possible to control imports and the rate of progress of the capital re-equipment, the convertibility of sterling caused a leakage of reserves which could not be controlled.

This was the time when the American Government had become convinced that the economic needs of Europe, including Great Britain, called for a large measure of direct assistance in addition to the loans which had been provided since the termination of Lend-Lease. The Committee of European Economic Co-operation, which had been con-

---

[1] The drawings on the Canadian credit are here expressed in U.S. dollars.

stituted to frame the response to General Marshall's epoch-making speech of the 5th June 1947, offering aid to Europe, was already in being. It was, therefore, with a lively sense of the urgency of the situation that the American Government agreed to a suspension of the convertibility of sterling, which took effect on the 20th August, after only six weeks' trial.

The flight from sterling into dollars is not to be attributed to fears of a diminished purchasing power of the pound. It was the dollar that was losing purchasing power; prices in terms of pounds were rising only because American prices were rising, and the pound was tied to the dollar by the fixed rate of exchange of $4·03. Yet the world undoubtedly regarded the dollar as pre-eminent and preferred the holding of dollars to the holding of pounds. The reason was that, while dollars were the means of acquiring American products and pounds were the means of acquiring British products, American products could be obtained promptly, and British products only after long delays.

How the combination of redundant money with urgent arrears of spending caused an excess demand for goods and over-employment of industry has been explained above (pp. 17–19). To this excess demand at home was added an excess demand abroad, for the foreign-held sterling, combined with an accumulated demand for imported manufactures in the countries which held it, intensified the pressure on British producers. There was no corresponding pressure on American exporters, for there had been no comparable accumulation of foreign-held dollar balances. The spending of dollars was unrestricted so far as American regulations were concerned and needy countries had quickly used up all the dollars they could spare.

So long as the British exchange control conformed to its wartime pattern, sterling held outside the Dollar Area and the Sterling Area could only be used to pay for imports by the holding country from the Sterling Area (or for its other current liabilities to the Sterling Area). Countries which held sterling in special accounts tended to encourage imports from the Sterling Area in order to use up their sterling. If imports into such a country were subject to quantitative restrictions, prices would be high, and attractive to the British exporter. The pressure of orders on British producers was so much the greater.

The breakdown of convertibility was due to the immediate advantages of the dollar over the pound as a medium for the purchase of supplies in world markets. At that time there was no important speculation against sterling. Amid the many uncertainties of the time, misgiving about the future of the British currency had not taken shape. But the breakdown itself gave a shock to confidence. The failure had been in dealing with the balance of payments. The resources at the disposal of the British Government for meeting the adverse balance had proved inadequate. That an adverse balance which cannot be met, and which is left to weigh on the market, depresses the foreign exchange value of the money unit was well recognised, was indeed self-evident. For the moment the abandonment of convertibility averted the threat to the pound, and the progress that was being made with the response to General Marshall's offer of aid to Europe held out the prospect of additional resources to meet adverse balances for several years to come. The last $300 million of the American loan was drawn out in the first quarter of 1948, but the first $89 million of Marshall Aid was received in the second quarter and $682 million followed in the second half of the year.

IMPORT RESTRICTIONS AND THE STERLING AREA

Apart from the intractable drain upon the monetary reserves caused by convertibility, the balance of payments could be kept in control by import restrictions. The Sterling Area would only admit imports to the amount that it could pay for. Theoretically, import restrictions should be a safeguard against an adverse balance, but in practice they are not easily adjusted with precision to changing requirements. While it is the total that has to be adjusted, each imported commodity has to be considered separately. Each has to be considered with reference not only to the needs of the home market but also to the rival claims of foreign suppliers, both the individual producers and the exporting countries. Any desired increase or decrease in the total quantity of imports has to be distributed among the various imported products, and in the case of each the interests affected have to be taken into account. And, when quantities have been decided on, the money value of the whole is liable to be altered by price movements.

Import restrictions work by trial and error. Error can only be estimated from the experience of a considerable period, probably several months, and the correction needed, when an error is revealed, can only be approximately estimated. Successive revisions, extending possibly over several years, may be necessary to arrive at a balance, and, before the adjustment is completed, new and unforeseen disturbing factors are likely enough to supervene.

In the case of Great Britain there are special complications. Over 80 per cent. of British imports consists of food and materials. Standards of nutrition do not allow the restriction of imported food supplies below a certain limit, and political considerations require whatever restriction is imposed to be effected mainly through rationing. The materials are to be used in industry. In so far as they are used in the production of goods for export, they are not final imports: their value is included in the proceeds of sale of the finished products, and a policy of import restriction is not applicable to them.[1] But it does apply to imported materials used in the production of goods for home consumption. If the supply of materials were cut down beyond a certain limit, the consequence would be not only austerity for the consumer but under-employment for the industries using the

---

[1] Except where materials paid for in hard currency are used in manufactures exported for soft currency.

materials. Post-war British Governments have reckoned the danger of unemployment being caused by a shortage of imported materials as one of their difficulties. The rise of the number of unemployed to 2,000,000 for a few days on account of the dislocation of the coal supply in 1947 is seen as an illustration of what might happen. Perhaps this fear at a time of intense over-employment in industry generally has been misconceived, or at any rate exaggerated, but it could not be altogether ignored.

But the greatest complication in the regulation of the British balance of payments by import restrictions has been the responsibility of Great Britain for the supply of foreign exchange to the rest of the Sterling Area. The essence of the Sterling Area, when given formal existence at the outbreak of war in 1939, was the freedom of transactions within it from exchange control. To make this freedom possible, the members had all to impose substantially the same exchange control on transactions with the outside world, and to adopt a common standard of import restrictions. They handed over whatever foreign exchange they earned from their trade with outside countries or otherwise to a central organisation, the British Exchange Equalisation Account administered by the Bank of England, and in return they were entitled to purchase the foreign exchange needed to pay for their imports. Any member which incurred an adverse balance through laxity in its import restrictions was helping itself from the monetary reserves of the whole Sterling Area. But there has not in general been any specific or systematic agreement as to the import restrictions each member is to impose.

Chapter Two

THE DEVALUATION OF 1949

The Dollar Balance, 1947–9

The adverse balance of the overseas Sterling Area with the Dollar Area rose from £73 million in 1946 to £306 million in 1947, and so much of the proceeds of the American and Canadian loans was used up in meeting it. In 1948 its adverse dollar balance subsided to £65 million, and that of Great Britain with the Dollar Area from £510 million to £252 million. The American loan was exhausted early in the year, but thereupon Marshall Aid (E.R.P.) took its place and sufficed to maintain a balance. From the 30th June 1948, when Marshall Aid first began to accrue in considerable amounts, to the 31st March 1949 the British monetary reserves remained at a nearly constant level.

The export drive was yielding results. By the beginning of 1949 exports from Great Britain were more than 50 per cent. above the pre-war volume. In 1948 the over-all adverse balance had been eliminated.

But that did not mean that the dollar problem was solved. In addition to the dollar deficits of £252 million incurred by Great Britain and £65 million by the rest of the Sterling Area, there were dollar liabilities on capital account of £66 million net, and dollar payments to non-dollar countries of £78 million, giving a total of £461 million, which was covered by the following resources (in £ millions):

American Loan	...	...	...	74
Canadian Loan	...	...	...	13
E.R.P. (Marshall Aid)		...	...	169
South African Gold Loan	...		...	80
Purchase of Sterling Area Gold			...	55
Drawn from International Monetary Fund		...	...	15
Drawn from reserves		...	...	55

461

It was especially in the second half of the year that the increase in exports was making itself felt, and of the £70 million drawn from the reserves and from the International Monetary Fund £54 million fell in the first half of the year and only £16 million in the second half.

For the time being controls seemed to have settled down in such a way as just to balance dollar requirements, and dollar resources. The excess of dollar requirements over the adverse balance of British trade as a whole constituted, of course, a favourable balance with the world outside the Dollar Area. This favourable balance was partly used up in investment in the Sterling Area and elsewhere, partly in a reduction of foreign-held sterling balances.[1]

The first quarter of 1949 continued the favourable showing of the second half of 1948. The dollar deficit of £72 million was more than covered by American Aid, along with £7½ million from the Canadian Loan, and reserves were increased by £14 million. But in the second quarter the deficit suddenly rose to £149 million, and reserves were drawn on to the amount of £65 million.

The failure of convertibility in 1947 had involved the British currency in some discredit. There was a loss of confidence in the future of the pound. Attention was concentrated on the balance of payments and the state of the

---

[1] The reduction of sterling balances was £174 million, but of this £150 million was accounted for by a capital transaction, the sale of the Argentine Railways.

reserves. A reserve reduced to £406 million (30th June 1949) could not long stand a drain at the rate of £65 million in three months.

THE DEVALUATION OF 1949

Even before the quarter was completed and the extent of the loss of reserves disclosed, there were signs of distrust. Irregular markets in pounds sterling had grown up in New York and other foreign centres, where transactions were beyond the jurisdiction of the British Exchange Control, and were not bound by official rates of exchange. 'Special Account' sterling could be converted into dollars at a price —a cargo, for instance, ostensibly destined for a soft-currency country and paid for from the appropriate special account, might be directed while in transit to be sold in a hard-currency country. When cargoes were bought at the high prices prevailing in soft-currency countries, the conversion into dollars meant some loss in comparison with the official rate of exchange. Consequently the irregular markets quoted sterling at a discount in terms of dollars.

It would not have been worth while to resort to such devices to procure dollars in exchange for sterling at a cost above the official price, unless there were some substantial reason for preferring dollars to sterling. The same reason existed as in 1947. British exporters were overloaded with orders and could only fulfil fresh orders at long delays. American exporters, having already in 1947 gone far towards emancipating themselves from the congestion of orders induced by price controls, had completed the process in the summer of 1948. The price level, as measured by the wholesale price index, reached a maximum in August 1948. Stocks of goods reached a maximum in November 1948.

American industry then had productive capacity to spare. In January 1949 the number of unemployed was 2,664,000, the highest since the war, and by July the number had risen to 4,095,000. The index of production of manufactures (100 in 1935–9) fell from 202 in October 1948 to 176 in June 1949. The increased advantage of American exporters in respect of promptitude of delivery was reflected in a growing discount on the pound in the irregular markets, and it was very natural to take this quotation as an indication of what the valuation of the pound would be in a free market if exchange control were abandoned. The idea, however, that a lowering of the official dollar value of the pound would be a step towards equilibrium was a dangerous misconception.

An adverse balance of payments working in markets free of all controls does automatically lower the foreign exchange value of the money unit, and under certain conditions tends towards equilibrium. It checks the consumption of imported goods by raising their prices. And it stimulates exports by offering them more favourable markets. If exports have previously been unremunerative owing to exporters' costs being excessive, a depreciation of the money unit which just makes them remunerative will enable the exporters to sell at international prices, and there is a clear gain in the country's exporting power. If producers are under-employed, as they were at the time of the suspension of the gold standard in 1931, additional exports can be produced without any reduction in production for home markets.

In 1949 conditions were totally different. Industry was suffering not from under-employment, but from over-employment. And the export trade was remunerative. Misgivings were sometimes expressed even in 1949 as to British exporters' costs being too high. And it is true that their prices were sometimes high; some exports were sold, under the shelter of the special account system, at inflated prices in soft-currency countries. But these prices were no evidence of *costs*. So far as the competition of American manufacturers was concerned, the dollar value of the pound had been reduced by one-fifth since 1938, and American wages had risen a little more than British.

When the foreign exchange value of the money unit is reduced below the level at which the export trade is normally remunerative, the effect on the balance of payments soon begins to be doubtful. The exporter does not necessarily sell at the same price in the foreign unit as before. He can extend his sales by selling at a lower price, which at the new rate of exchange may still be higher in terms of his own money unit. To a manufacturer an extension of his sales is likely to be attractive, while he may feel some compunction against asking a price which will yield him an exorbitant profit.

Depreciation of the unit thus induces an expansion of exports, but only at the cost of a reduction of export prices in terms of foreign money units. There is no certainty that the increase in quantity will be sufficient to compensate the decrease of price: there may thus be no increase and possibly an actual decrease in the total proceeds of exports in terms of foreign money. That is especially likely to happen when the productive capacity of industry is already fully employed.

In 1949 British industry was not merely fully employed but over-employed. It was only with difficulty that a producer for export could obtain the necessary resources for extending his output: for labour he would be bidding in a market where demand exceeded supply; for additional equipment he would be competing against orders which already strained the productive capacity of suppliers.

Depreciation of the money unit raises the prices of imports and discourages demand for them. But in 1949 imports into Great Britain were subject to prohibitions, quantitative restrictions, rationing and other controls, so that price had little to do with determining demand. Imports had been reduced nearly to a minimum, so that a depreciation of the pound could not reduce them much further. If depreciation actually diminished the aggregate proceeds of exports, there was evidently a danger that a vicious circle would be set up. An adverse balance of payments would cause a depreciation of the pound, and depreciation would make the balance still more adverse. To rely on a free rate of exchange as a corrective would be to open the door to an indefinite process of depreciation and a monetary collapse.

One of the conditions of American aid under the European Recovery Programme was that the recipients should maintain 'valid rates of exchange'. And anyhow the United States, while contributing funds which, however their purpose might be described, were in fact supporting European currencies, could obviously claim a say in the policies determining the rates of exchange of which support was to be given. Opinion in American financial and political circles quite failed to appreciate the complexities of the British monetary situation. Since the British authorities had failed to maintain equilibrium in the balance of payments, then they must have failed to maintain a valid rate of exchange, and the conclusion was drawn that they ought to reduce the dollar value of the pound. In the spring of 1949, just when the British Government was putting out estimates showing that the British share of Marshall Aid would be insufficient, the United States Congress cut down the appropriation for Marshall Aid. Its action was symptomatic of the view which was becoming prevalent in America that the British were causing their own difficulties by clinging to an overvaluation of the pound. If this was a misreading of the situation, it was surely for the British authorities to resist it, and to make a reasoned reply. But they seem to have seen no further into the real causes of their troubles than the Americans.

Their first action, after the unfavourable results of the quarter ending June 1949 were disclosed, had been to impose more severe import restrictions, and to obtain the agreement of their partners in the Sterling Area to similar measures. But the new restrictions could affect the adverse balance only after an interval of time, and meanwhile the loss of reserves was being aggravated by a speculative movement against sterling. There had arisen a general expectation that the official dollar-sterling rate of exchange would soon be reduced below the rate of $4·03 which had prevailed since September 1939. Intending importers from the Ster-

D

ling Area delayed ordering goods in the hope that they would soon be able to pay for them in devalued pounds. Intending exporters to the Sterling Area hastened deliveries of their goods and the exchange of the sterling they received into their own money. Against this speculative movement there was no resistance. If the British Government and their advisers had in their minds any reason whatever why devaluation of the pound should not take place, they omitted to mention it. At the end of August they decided to reduce the dollar value of the pound from $4·03 to $2·80. The decision was not given immediate effect. Consultations followed with the American and Canadian Governments, and with the International Monetary Fund, and then on the 18th September the devaluation was formally announced.

The devaluation, amounting to 30·5 per cent., was far greater than had been anticipated. It was great enough to dispel any expectations of a further reduction of value in the near future, and thereby gained the immediate advantage of a reversal of the speculative movement against sterling. The monetary reserves which had fallen from $1,651 million at the end of June 1949 to $1,340 million on the 18th September, recovered to $1,425 million on the 30th September and $1,688 million on the 31st December. On the 31st March 1950 the reserves stood at $1,984 million, and were above the level of March 1949, and the increase was still continuing.

The effects of the reversal of the speculation cannot be supposed to have continued far into 1950. But the import restrictions imposed in July 1949 began to take effect. The intention then announced of reducing imports from the Dollar Area into Great Britain from $1,600 million a year to $1,200 million was precisely fulfilled. These imports had been, in 1948 $1,634 million, and in the first half of 1949 $829 million. The restrictions took some time to be reflected in the statistics, and the second half of 1949 recorded only a moderate reduction to $777 million. But the imports in the year 1950 were $1,206 million. British exports to the Dollar

Area had shown no appreciable change in the first half of 1949. In the second half they fell to $318 million comparing with $393 million in the first half and with $792 million in the whole year 1948. The recovery in 1950 to $907 million was partly attributable to the reversal of the speculative movement against sterling, which had delayed orders for British exports in 1949; the export markets were making good arrears of supplies. But whereas the total dollar value of exports to the Dollar Area had risen by nearly 15 per cent., the volume had risen by 45 per cent.[1] The sterling price level of these exports had risen in the proportion of 88 to 100, but their dollar price level had fallen in the proportion of 88 to 69½, or by 21 per cent.

The adverse balance of the overseas Sterling Area with the Dollar Area had been $263 million in 1948, and was somewhat higher at $173 million in the first half of 1949. In the second half it fell to $86 million, and the first half of 1950 recorded a favourable balance of $200 million, which was increased in the second half to $273 million. As in the case of Great Britain, the gain was mainly through a reduction of imports. The *Balance of Payments* White Paper (Cmd. 8976, p. 69) gives statistics of the transactions of the overseas Sterling Area with the Dollar Area, and the following table shows (in $ millions) the exports and imports (exclusive of those of the Union of South Africa, which retains its dollar settlements in its own hands).

TABLE II

	Imports from Dollar Area	Exports to Dollar Area	Balance
1948 ...	1,185	1,140	− 45
1949: 1st Half	605	510	− 95
2nd Half	420	395	− 25
1950: 1st Half	380	550	+170
2nd Half	345	670	+325
1951: 1st Half	535	1,040	+505
2nd Half	780	605	−175

[1] *Board of Trade Journal*, 1st August, 1953, p. 220.

The second half of 1950 begins to reflect the rise of prices of primary products which ensued upon the outbreak of the Korean War (see below, pp. 48–9). But the most pertinent comment on the statistics seems to be that the adverse movement which provoked the crisis was a very limited affair. But for the speculation against sterling, which for a time exaggerated the effects of the shrinkage of demand in the Dollar Area for exports from both Great Britain and the rest of the Sterling Area, it need hardly have caused a moment's anxiety.

INFLATION AND DEFLATION IN THE UNITED STATES, 1946–9

The trouble originated in American conditions. For more than two years from the summer of 1946 American industry was adapting itself to the abandonment of controls. The rise of prices was a symptom of an expansion of demand, measured by the rise of the national income from $173,500 million in the middle of 1946 to $234,300 million at the end of 1948. The monetary system of Great Britain, like those of most of the rest of the world, was tied to the American by the fixed rate of exchange with the dollar. The expansion of demand in America was reflected in the increase of British exports to the Dollar Area from $404 million in 1946 to $523 million in 1947 and $792 million in 1948. Concurrently there was a big demand for materials of industry, which was felt by the primary producers of the Sterling Area. As we saw above, stocks of goods in America had been replenished by the end of 1948, and thereupon the state of exceptional activity came to an end. With the consequent decline of demand American imports fell from a quarterly average of $1,781 million in 1948 to $1,590 million in the second quarter and $1,501 million in the third quarter of 1949.

The pound had been linked to the dollar by the fixed rate of $4·03 when the dollar was losing value by reason of the American inflation of 1946–8. If it was to remain so linked

when the inflation was reversed in 1949, the classic corrective would have been a contraction of credit. But deflation
had become odious and was not contemplated. It would
have been denounced as a method of transplanting unemployment from America to England.

The special circumstances of British industry at the time
were not appreciated. In its then existing state of over-
employment it could have stood a substantial measure of
credit contraction without developing unemployment. The
first impact would be to relieve the burden of unfilled orders.

Nor did the situation require a monetary contraction so
severe as to force a reduction of British wages and prices.
In view of the heavy fall in the dollar equivalent of British
wages relative to American wages since 1938, it might fairly
be contended that even at $4·03 the pound was under-
valued, and that its under-valuation was a contributory
cause of the over-employment. If so, the monetary contraction required would have been no more than sufficient
to correct the over-employment.

In the absence of any restrictive monetary policy, the
resort to more severe import restrictions in July 1949 was
unavoidable. The country could not be allowed to go on
buying imports which it could not pay for.

In any appraisal of the situation in 1949, much depended
on the immediate prospect in the United States. The recession that was in progress might turn out to be transitory or
it might be the prelude to a severe and prolonged depression.
If the former, it could be tided over by drawing on reserves,
or, should they be insufficient, a restriction of imports
would be a tolerable stop-gap expedient. If the latter, there
might be so heavy a decline in the American price level as to
make British costs really excessive.

The conditions in the United States pointed very clearly
to an early recovery of activity. The redundant money
which had set going the expansion and rise of prices of
1946–8 had not been entirely eliminated.[1] And, what was

[1] The proportion of money to a year's national income had fallen to 75·7 in 1948,
or very near the 73·5 of 1941. But it was still above normal.

more important, the policy of easy credit still prevailed and the support of the market in Government securities by the Federal Reserve Bank meant that reserves of these securities could be practically treated as cash. The budget surpluses of 1947 and 1948 had given place to a moderate deficit in 1949; the national debt and the commercial banks' holdings of Government securities were increasing. Ostensibly the dollar was on a gold standard equating an ounce of fine gold to $35. But with a gold reserve exceeding $24,000 million (equivalent to more than three years' imports) there was no question of gold putting any impediment in the way of a monetary expansion. The value of gold was determined by the value of the dollar, not that of the dollar by that of gold.

Before the end of 1949 American industrial production was recovering and the volume of imports (though not the value) was higher than in 1948. By June 1950 the index of industrial production was higher than at any time in 1948, and the volume of imports had further increased and was increasing. Thus the conditions which had caused the adverse dollar balance of the Sterling Area in the summer of 1949 turned out to be transitory, and the import restrictions imposed in July were sufficient to tide them over.

IMPORT RESTRICTIONS AND CONSUMPTION

A restriction of imports may be either a temporary or permanent measure. If it is to be a permanent measure it must bring about a reduction in the *consumption* of imported products. Then the curtailment of imports can last as long as the curtailment of consumption. If, on the other hand, there is no curtailment of consumption, the restriction of imports is reflected in a reduction of the stocks held of the imported goods. If consumption is to be maintained undiminished, then when stocks have shrunk to a minimum, there must be imports equal to consumption. If stocks are to be restored to normal, imports must exceed consumption.

It is significant that in 1950, when the restriction of imports took full effect, there was a reduction in volume of stocks of £183 million, and in 1951 there was an increase of £506 million (additions to the value of stocks through the rise of prices being eliminated in both instances). Evidently the restriction imposed in July 1949 is to be counted a temporary measure. It did not involve 'austerity' and there was in fact a slight increase of consumption in 1950, an increase all in stock-held products, not in services.[1]

The restriction of imports, even if continued beyond the stage at which it could be absorbed in a reduction of stocks, would not have been deemed an acceptable permanent policy. The imported superfluities which could easily be dispensed with had long been excluded. If restrictions meant either a more severe rationing of food or an allocation of materials to industry so restricted as to cause under-employment of capacity and unemployment of labour, they would evidently be undesirable.

On a longer view the British balance of payments in 1949 was beset by threats of future weakness. The American aid by which the adverse balance was being supported was being scrutinised by Congress in a very grudging spirit, and was in any case due to end in 1952. Even with that aid it had been found necessary to tighten the import restrictions. There was evident need of some permanently effective remedial measures.

An adverse balance is a symptom of too much spending, spending to be understood in the wide sense to include spending on capital formation as well as on consumption.[2]

We have seen (above, p. 17) how the combination of accumulations of redundant money with arrears of necessary outlays caused an intense pressure to spend, and how the Government relied on controls and measures of austerity to resist this pressure. Up to a point import restrictions were a part of the system of controls: restriction of spending

[1] See *National Income and Expenditure*, 1946–52, Table 17.
[2] An adverse balance may be caused by a flight of capital, which may not be spending on the formation of new capital, but on the purchase of existing capital assets abroad. The flight of capital, however, usually occurs only after an adverse balance caused by excessive spending has gone so far as to cause distrust of the money.

included restriction of spending on imported goods. Import restrictions beyond that point were an emergency measure, taken to prevent a breakdown when controls failed to keep down spending and the consequent adverse balance threatened to exhaust the reserves.

A permanent remedy might be looked for in intensified controls, in which import restrictions would continue to play their part. But controls had been found wanting. There was no control of wages. Rationing could only cover a part of the ground. Price control, if it limited spending in terms of money units, left demand unsatisfied, and the pressure to spend intensified.

REDUNDANT MONEY AND MONETARY POLICY

These shortcomings may or may not have been officially recognised, but experience itself did not encourage reliance on controls. Something better was desired to serve as a long-term policy.

The pressure to spend, which was the root of the trouble, was due to the combination of arrears of spending with redundant money, and, it may be added, with easy credit. Spending presupposes a supply of money; spending in excess of income presupposes a supply of money in excess of that received by way of income. If the supply of money is cut short, the spending becomes impossible.

The consumers' income is primarily applicable to consumption. Saving, the excess of incomes over consumption, is available to meet capital outlay. It takes the form partly of reinvested profits of business concerns, partly of sums accruing from individual incomes. The sums accruing to individuals are applied to capital outlay, partly by being directly spent upon building houses or improving property for themselves, partly by being placed in the investment market, where they supply the resources for business concerns which raise capital from the market by flotations or sales of securities.

Capital outlay may exceed saving (and, therefore, spending exceed income) through consumers placing sums in excess of their savings in the investment market (either from balances or from borrowed money) or through dealers in the investment market supplementing their resources with borrowed money, or through traders supplementing the funds raised from the investment market and from re-invested profits by bank advances.

Thus spending in excess of income cannot proceed unless it is fed either from existing cash balances or from bank advances. Excess spending can be prevented, and therefore an adverse balance of payments avoided, by sufficiently severe checks upon the supply of money.

The classical remedy of 'dear money', high short-term rates of interest, discourages borrowing from the banks. By causing a diminution of bank advances, it brings about a contraction in bank assets and therefore in bank deposits, that is to say, in the supply of money.

But if the supply of money is in excess of requirements, the classical remedy may fail to be effective, for people who can spend from their own surplus balances do not need to borrow, and even those who have no surplus balances may be able to raise money from others who have money to spare and need not have recourse to the banks.

It was such considerations that led me to write, while the war was still going on, that 'the machinery of bank rate and reserves of foreign exchange, which works well enough in quiet times, is only too likely to prove inadequate to cope with the accumulated force of the inflationary finance of several years of war.'[1] And I then suggested, as a post-war measure, a forced loan assessed on holdings of currency and bank deposits, accompanied by credit restriction in the form of dear money and any other suitable measures, in order to prevent the money extinguished from being replaced through bank advances creating fresh credit.

So exceptional a device as a forced loan would have been

[1] *Economic Destiny* (1944), p. 243. See also my *Economic Rebirth* (1946), pp. 47–50.

warranted by the magnitude of the operation. When I wrote, it was already evident that the redundant money would amount to thousands of millions. If the holders could be induced to prefer a permanent investment in Government funded or long-dated stock to ready cash, the ordinary mechanism of a loan floated in the investment market without compulsion would have served the purpose. But the redundant money was for the most part in the hands of people who had involuntarily postponed expenditure in consequence of war conditions, and who would not part with their money on any terms, but would retain it in order to discharge their arrears of spending as soon as those conditions were relaxed.

In 1949 conditions had in some degree changed. There was still redundant money, but owing to the increased flow of money, its proportion had decreased. The gross national production increased from £8,662 million in 1946 to £10,926 million in 1949, or 26 per cent., while the supply of money increased by less than 10 per cent. Several years of capital outlay, assisted by the American and Canadian loans and Marshall Aid, had made some impression on the arrears of spending. It is possible that a substantial amount of redundant money could be extinguished by the issue of funded or long-term securities which would have been acquired as a permanent investment.

Bank advances were still relatively low. But they reached £1,378 million at the end of 1948, and increased in the course of 1949 to £1,504 million. The ratio to deposits, about 25 per cent., was far below the 40 per cent. or so which had been usual before the war (50 per cent. in 1929), but still was high enough to provide some scope for a policy of dear money.

The way, in fact, was open to restraining the excess spending, and so removing the danger of an adverse balance, by monetary measures—had it not been for the political prejudice against any such course.

No doubt it was partly reluctance to contemplate dear

money and credit restriction that turned the searches of the Government in the direction of the rate of exchange. The fixed rate of exchange of $4.03 committed the pound to following the fluctuations in the purchasing power of the dollar. So long as the American price level was rising, so that the dollar was losing value, it was easy to indulge in an inflationary tendency corresponding to that which was at work in the United States: no effort was called for in dropping away to leeward. But if a setback to the expansion in the United States demanded a spell of beating to windward, the fixed rate of exchange became less attractive.

THE INTERNATIONAL MONETARY FUND

It was the International Monetary Fund, agreed on at Bretton Woods, that made the American dollar the monetary standard for the rest of the world. The dollar is an unstable unit, subject to alternations of rising and falling purchasing power, which its link with gold fails to modify. A money unit which follows the dollar at a fixed rate when it is losing value, but detaches itself when the dollar is gaining value, will be subject to progressive depreciation. To escape from the dilemma of progressive depreciation on the one hand and recurrent spells of deflation on the other, it would be necessary to raise the dollar value of the money unit when the American price level is rising, and to lower its dollar value when the American price level is falling. But that would be contrary to the principles of the International Monetary Fund, unless the fluctuations in the dollar were deemed to constitute an almost continuous series of states of 'fundamental disequilibrium'.

Even the policy of reducing the dollar value of the money unit every time the wealth-value of the dollar rises is almost as irreconcilable with the principles established for the Fund. For the rise in the wealth-value of the dollar would occur gradually over a period of months or years, and the extent of the rise ultimately to be dealt with could not be foreseen. A series of tentative adjustments of the rate of exchange would be needed.

There was no explicit acceptance of any such policy in 1949. It has deserved mention because it is implied in two assumptions: that the dollar value of the pound must remain fixed except in the case of a fundamental dis-equilibrium; and that there must be no deflation.

The measures taken in the period 1946–9 were a very equivocal application of this policy. During the phase of American inflation up to 1948 the British wage-level and price-level increased by 20 per cent. and 27 per cent., while the American increased by 29 per cent. and 50 per cent. The setback in 1949 caused a fall of 11 per cent. in the American price-level and no fall at all in the wage level. It might reasonably have been expected that the lag of British costs and prices behind the rise in American costs and prices would provide a margin to cover this rise in the wealth-value of the dollar.

The devaluation actually decided on took no account at all of these considerations. It is not even to be understood as providing against a more serious American setback. An appreciation of the dollar of such magnitude as to justify a devaluation of 30·5 per cent. would point to a depression comparable to that of 1929–32, when the American price index fell from 95·2 to 63·9, or 33 per cent. It may be that the precedent of 1931 was not altogether absent from the minds of the British authorities. But that does not mean that they were anticipating a violent monetary contraction in the United States, but rather that they interpreted the adverse balance with the Dollar Area as evidence that the costs of British producers and exporters were excessive, in spite of the fact that since 1946 American wages had been rising relatively more than British.

That the true cause of the weakness of the pound was not excessive costs but the over-employment and delayed deliveries of British industry was quickly demonstrated. Had excessive costs been the cause, devaluation would have been the remedy. But, as it turned out, within a week of the devaluation the irregular market in New York was quoting the pound at a discount on the new rate of exchange of $2·80.

PRICES AFTER DEVALUATION

Devaluation did of course give exporters an increased competitive advantage in respect of costs, not only in their exports to the Dollar Area, but in their exports to any market which was supplied in competition with them from the Dollar Area. They found an increased demand at a given sterling price, and an increased demand even at a higher sterling price, so long as the equivalent of the higher sterling price was a lower dollar price. But the increased demand actually intensified the over-employment which was their most substantial competitive disadvantage. Productive capacity for additional exports had to be diverted from other uses where demand was also intense.

The export drive had already raised the volume of exports (to all destinations) in 1949 to 151·6 per cent. of that of 1938. In 1950 there was a further increase to 174·3, or by 15 per cent. But the average export price level rose only 5 per cent., so that the dollar value of total exports *fell* by 27 per cent.

There were, of course, many export markets in which dollar prices had little relevance, and a great part of British imports were from countries which had also devalued their money units, and where prices had not risen in proportion to the devaluation, if at all. A great part of the imports had, therefore, risen relatively little in price, and some were being procured under Governmental bulk purchase agreements at contractual prices settled before devaluation. Average import prices were 14 per cent. higher in 1950 than in 1949. Had the prices of exports risen by 14 per cent. instead of by 5 per cent., they would have been valued at £2,426 million instead of £2,247 million. Devaluation resulted in British exports being sold too cheap, and the un-favourable terms of trade added some £180 million to the adverse balance of payments.

The pricing of manufactured products differs from that of primary products. It is usual for the manufacturer to quote his own price when offered an order, and his starting point is a calculation of his costs and a reasonable margin of profit. He may quote a lower price than that so calculated, if his plant is under-employed and he has to face competition from rival producers who will cut prices in order to get orders. He is not so likely to quote a higher price, yielding him more than a reasonable profit, when the state of the market is favourable. From time immemorial an excessive profit has been thought something to be ashamed of, and likely to invite censure from customers and from public opinion, if it gets known. It is also apt to lead to demands from the workpeople employed for higher wages.

The producer of primary products (foodstuffs, organic materials or minerals) recognises no such close relation between price and costs. His price in fact covers economic rent as well as profit. His price also is speculative and highly variable. The demand for materials is governed by the demand for the finished products, and as the cost of materials is usually only a small fraction of the cost of the finished products, the demand for a finished product is very unresponsive to variations in the prices of the materials embodied in it.

And whereas a manufacturer endeavours to suit his product to the requirements of the purchaser who orders it, the characteristics of a primary product are principally deter-mined by the natural conditions in which it is produced. The world's primary products are to a great extent pooled for sale in world markets, where they command competitive prices. The individual producer bargains to receive the world price appropriate to his product.

British exports are nearly all manufactured goods, and did not easily take advantage of the opportunity which

devaluation afforded of raising prices. The 6 per cent. rise
in 1950 cannot have much exceeded the additional cost of
imported materials used in producing the exported goods.
The 'added cost' of manufacture must have been practically
unchanged.

British imports on the other hand were mostly primary
products, and a great part of them rose in price in proportion to the rise in the sterling value of the dollar. The
14 per cent. rise in the prices of imports in 1950 was a long
way short of the rise of 44 per cent. in the sterling value of
the dollar.[1] But most of the money units outside the Dollar
Area had been devalued along with sterling (some, however,
such as France, Italy, Germany and Belgium in a smaller
proportion), and it was possible to maintain many purchasing agreements, for a time, with little or no alteration of
prices.

There were, of course, tendencies at work to correct the
unfavourable terms of trade. Under conditions of over-
employment, manufacturers for export would find themselves unable to expand their output, and would soon be
tempted to raise their prices. High profits, combined with
an intense demand for labour, would be favourable ground
for claims for higher wages, and higher wages would both
underpin the prices already raised and cause other prices to
rise in proportion to costs.

But a rise of wages and therefore of costs would directly
conflict with the policy of reducing costs by devaluation.
And the Government, after the devaluation of 1949, pressed
strongly for a standstill of wages, at any rate for a year. To
this the leaders of organised labour, with suitable reserva-
tions, agreed, and the index of weekly wages (100 in 1947)
rose only from 109 in 1949 to 111 in 1950. As American
wages (hourly earnings) increased by $4\frac{1}{2}$ per cent. less than
no progress was being made towards correcting the effect
of devaluation on the terms of trade.

[1] $\dfrac{4\cdot03}{2\cdot80} = 1\cdot44$

Chapter Three

ARMAMENTS AND NATIONAL FINANCE

KOREA AND PRICES OF MATERIALS

IN June 1950 the Korean War broke out. There ensued a big increase in the expenditure on armaments in both America and Europe, and, even before that increase began, a sensational rise in the prices of materials, due partly to the prospective demands of the armament industries, but more directly to the policy of accumulating strategic stocks. The price index of American imports of materials (100 in 1936–1938) having fallen from 206 in the first quarter of 1949 to 185 in the first quarter of 1950, rose to 215 in the third quarter and 255 in the fourth. It reached a maximum of 340 in the second quarter of 1951, and thereafter fell throughout 1952.

American imports of materials may be taken to be a sample from world markets, and the rise in dollar prices aggravated the adverse terms of trade for Great Britain. The sterling value of British imports of raw materials from all sources rose from £690 million in 1949 and £960 million in 1950 to £1,572 million in 1951. (Other imports were £1,288 million, £1,418 million and £1,924 million.)

In contrast with a favourable over-all balance of payments on current account of £298 million in 1950 there was an adverse balance of £410 million in 1951. The dollar balance was a credit of £308 million in 1950, a further credit of £154 million in the first half of 1951, but a debit of £561 million in the second half.

The reserve of gold and dollars rose from £603 million at the end of 1949 to £1,178 million at the end of 1950. The rise was continuing and brought the reserve to £1,381 million in June 1951. This favourable showing led the Government to announce, in 1950, that no more American aid would be needed after the end of that year, apart from the receipt of what was already on order. The aid received in 1950 had been £252 million. In the first half of 1951 it was only £49 million and in the second half £14 million.

The cessation of American aid accounted for but a small part of the loss of dollars and gold, which reduced the monetary reserve from £1,381 million on the 30th June 1951 to £834 million on the 31st December. The loss was the resultant of several different factors. The high prices of materials (especially of wool, rubber and tin) had yielded the overseas Sterling Area a surplus of £162 million in its trade with the Dollar Area in the first half of 1951. The fall of prices converted the surplus into a debit of £59 million in the second half.

The table on p. 35 above, shows that the reversal was attributable to increased imports as well as to decreased proceeds of exports. The following continuation of the table shows (in $ millions) that imports reached a maximum in the first half of 1952, and fell heavily in the following twelve months, whereas exports were approximately stabilised.

TABLE III

	Imports from Dollar Area	Exports to Dollar Area	Balance
1948 ...	1,185	1,140	− 45
1949 ...	1,025	905	− 120
1950 ...	725	1,220	+495
1951: 1st Half	535	1,040	+505
2nd Half	780	605	− 175
1952: 1st Half	830	685	− 145
2nd Half	530	605	+ 75
1953: 1st Half	425	605	+180

It was the swollen exports of the first half of 1951 that led to the relaxation of import restrictions; and the increased

E

debit for imports accrued in the second half of the year and the first half of 1952. The imports in the twelve months ending June 1952 amounted to $1,610 million, whereas exports were only $1,290 million.

Nor had the import restrictions in Great Britain itself been maintained. The institution of the European Payments Union had been associated with an agreement by members of the Organisation for European Economic Co-operation (O.E.E.C.) for the liberalisation of their trade with one another, that is to say, for the gradual removal of import restrictions and similar impediments. In 1949 the volume of British imports from all sources had still been at a low level, about 85 per cent. of that of 1938. The restrictions imposed in 1949, though they reduced dollar imports, left the total volume of imports in 1950 unchanged at 85 per cent. (100 in 1938), and even so stocks of goods were reduced. In 1951 the volume of imports rose by one-eighth to 96 per cent. and there was a big addition to stocks. In the second half of the year the accounts of the European Payments Union disclosed a series of heavy debits against Great Britain, of which £91 million had to be met in gold.

Among the adverse factors mention may be made of the interest and sinking funds of the American and Canadian loans, payment of which began at the end of 1951, and the loss of profit sustained by the Anglo-Iranian Oil Company through the cancellation of its concession in Persia.

ARMAMENTS AND TAXATION

Great Britain had to take up its share of the increased expenditure on armaments which followed on the outbreak of the Korean War. Defence expenditure in 1949 was £762 million. The increase in 1950 was moderate, bringing the total to £810 million, but in 1951 defence expenditure rose to £1,086 million, in addition to £127 million spent on strategic stocks of materials.

The budget of 1951–2 made substantial additions to direct taxation. The additional tax on wages and salaries began to be collected immediately. But the income tax and surtax, so far as they are imposed on profits of business concerns, do not come in course of payment till after the 1st January following the budget, so that the additional taxes imposed in the budget of 1951 did not begin to be paid till the 1st January 1952.

A company whose accounting period is the calendar year knows that it will begin to pay tax on the profits of the year twelve months after the end of the year. The tax of 1951 is assessed on the profits of 1950, and is paid in 1952. Prudence requires it to set aside a reserve in its balance sheet against the prospective tax liability. The reserve has to cover two years' tax: that figuring in the balance sheet of 31st December 1951 includes both the ascertained tax already assessed on the profits of 1950, and about to become due for payment after the 1st January 1952, and also the estimated tax on the profits of 1951. The latter tax will not have to be paid till 1953, but the financial arrangements of the company must provide for it in due course.

Therefore, though the additional taxes of 1951 did not have to be paid till 1952, the money required was tied up in tax reserves in 1951. The actual payment of taxes on profits rose from £1,180 million in 1951 to £1,418 million in 1952. But the additions to tax reserves in 1951 amounted to £536 million, and this large total reflected the increased tax liability on the current profits to be assessed in 1952 for payment in 1953, as well as on those already assessed for payment in 1952. The actual payments of income tax and profits tax on profits and interest year by year, together with the additions to tax reserves, are shown (in £ millions) in the table on the following page.

In the year 1946 there were substantial reductions of taxation. Income tax was reduced from 10s. in the pound to 9s., and the Excess Profits Tax from 100 per cent. (subject to post-war credit of 20) to 60 per cent., and was to expire after 31st December 1946. No doubt the reduction of £72 million in tax reserves was less than it would have been but for the tendency of incomes and profits to rise.

TABLE IV

	1946	1947	1948	1949	1950	1951	1952
Income Tax	654	596	655	781	808	788	946
Surtax	55	60	76	85	87	95	97
Profits Tax and Excess Profits Tax	391	286	283	300	277	297	375
	1,100	942	1,014	1,166	1,172	1,180	1,418
Addition to Tax Reserves	−72	212	163	12	126	536	120
	1,028	1,154	1,177	1,178	1,298	1,716	1,538

In the following five years, 1947–51, the total of the additions to tax reserves was £1,049 million. The reserves had to cover double the increase in the annual amount of taxation payable out of profits over the amount in the year 1947. The addition to tax reserves in 1947 was designed to provide for the taxes to be collected in 1948 and 1949 on the profits which had accrued up to 1947. The further additions up to the end of 1951 provided for taxes on the profits up to the end of that year which would be payable in 1952 and later. The taxes collected in 1952 exceeded by £391 million those collected in 1948. The addition to tax reserves was much more than double that sum, but a large additional tax burden was pending after 1952. The budget of 1951 provided big prospective increases of taxation, which would not take effect in the immediately ensuing financial year. In particular the suspension of initial allowances of extra depreciation on new capital outlay, incurred after 6th April 1952, which was expected to gain £170 million to the revenue in a full year, could not take effect till the profits earned from April 1952 onwards were actually charged to income tax. Tax would only begin to be paid in 1954, but

tax reserves would be provided not only in 1952 but in 1951
when capital outlay would be planned months ahead, and
finance provided for it.

Tax reserves, not being available for distribution as dividends, are a form of reinvested profits. In the interval before
they are required for payment of taxes they may be used in
diminution of temporary borrowing, or, if that is not
needed, they may be held in cash or in short-term investments (such as tax-reserve certificates which amounted to
£367 million on the 31st March 1952, immediately after the
year's principal payment of income tax). The big addition
of £536 million to tax reserves in 1951 was the equivalent
of an additional budget surplus in its effect on capital
resources.

The budget of 1951 did better than had been estimated,
the surplus realised on the financial year 1951–2 being £380
million in place of the £39 million budgeted for. In the
calendar year 1951 (including the last quarter of the financial year 1950–1, when re-armament had hardly begun) the
surplus amounted to £628 million. The surplus (subject to
some adjustments, e.g., for part being derived from capital
taxes) was a contribution to the country's savings. The
budget of 1951, by adding £536 millions of tax reserves to
this surplus, provided capital resources exceeding £1,000
million. Was this not a sufficient provision against excess
spending?

The position was not so favourable as appears on the
surface. The years 1950 and 1951 had seen a great rise of
prices, which was reflected in the valuation of stocks of
goods. When the value of a trader's stock rises, the incre-
ment of value counts as profit for the purposes of taxation.
But the stock is part of his capital, and, so long as he holds
it, the profit derived from the rise of price is tied up in it: it
is part of his reinvested profits. He may have turned over his
stock several times in the course of the year, and so have
realised the greater part of the profit in cash. But, unless he
is in a position to reduce the amount of stock held, he has

to use all the cash, including the profit, in the latest purchases for the replenishment of stock.

Consequently the money for payment of tax on this part of his profit must be found from the rest of his resources, and the amount of his disposable profits, whether for distribution as dividends or for the accumulation of undistributed profits in reserves, is so much the less.

In the two years 1950 and 1951 the value of stocks held rose by £1,823 million, of which no less than £1,500 million represented the rise of prices, the balance of £323 million being an increase in quantity. Payment of tax on this large sum (composed of £700 million in 1950 and £800 million in 1951) was a serious encroachment on the taxpayers' disposable savings.

To elucidate the position a short statistical survey of the relation between capital resources, stocks and the balance of payments will be helpful.

CAPITAL FORMATION AND RESOURCES

Capital formation is composed of two parts: capital outlay and additions to stocks. The Central Statistical Office, in the Return of National Income and Expenditure, calls capital outlay Fixed Capital Formation, but the term 'Fixed' is not appropriate to vehicles, ships, and movable plant and tools, which are not legally 'fixtures'. It could be more accurately called Instrumental Capital Formation, but Capital Outlay is a more concise and convenient description. It must be understood (as it can quite properly) to exclude the purchase of goods for stock, destined for resale (with or without processing) as not being a final outlay.

A remarkable characteristic of the British economic structure since the war has been the steadiness of the total amount of capital outlay. The following table sets out (in millions of pounds) the yearly amount of capital outlay and its equivalent at the price level of 1948.

TABLE V
Capital Outlay

				Actual	At Prices of 1948
1946	...	...	...	900	1,025
1947	...	...	...	1,160	1,259
1948	...	...	...	1,393	1,393
1949	...	...	...	1,534	1,491
1950	...	...	...	1,674	1,562
1951	...	...	...	1,863	1,545
1952	...	...	...	2,054	1,551

The big increase from 1946 to 1949 reflects the return from war to peace conditions. Since then the rise in actual capital outlay has been attributable to a fall in the wealth value of money and there has been no appreciable increase in volume. By contrast the considerable fluctuations in capital formation as a whole are shown in the following table (in £ millions) to be due to variations in stocks of goods.

TABLE VI
Capital Formation

	Capital Outlay	Increase in Stocks			Capital Formation
		Total	Due to Price	Due to Volume	
1946	900	138	150	− 12	888
1947	1,160	828	450	378	1,538
1948	1,393	538	325	213	1,606
1949	1,534	290	225	65	1,599
1950	1,674	517	700	− 183	1,491
1951	1,863	1,306	800	506	2,369
1952	2,054	− 115	50	− 165	1,889

In the last column the increase in the value of stocks due to price is excluded, as only the increase in volume is regarded as contributing to capital formation.

The surplus war stores and the strategic stocks held by the Government are not part of the stocks forming the country's working capital. Therefore, the proceeds of sale of surplus war stores (Table 28, Item 6c, in the *Return of National Income and Expenditure, 1946–52*) have been added to the yearly increase in volume (Table 6, Item 5) and the cost of strategic stocks (Table 28, Item 6b) has been deducted.

The National Income Return (p. viii) gives estimates of total capital formation at the prices of 1948. A proportional adjustment of the increase in stocks, to allow for Government sales of surplus war stores and purchases of strategic stocks, gives the following results (in £ millions):

TABLE VII
Capital Formation at Prices of 1948

		Capital Outlay	Increase in Stocks	Capital Formation
1946	...	1,025	− 15	1,010
1947	...	1,259	396	1,655
1948	...	1,393	213	1,606
1949	...	1,491	59	1,550
1950	...	1,562	−159	1,403
1951	...	1,545	376	1,921
1952	...	1,551	−122	1,429

Stocks at the end of 1951 (exclusive of Government-held strategic stocks and surplus) were £7,258 million. The total additions at current values in the six years 1946–51 were £3,617 million, so that the stocks at the beginning of 1946 were £3,641 million. The net additions at the prices of 1948 were £870 million. Recalculated at the prices of 1946 they come to £793 million, representing an increase in volume of 22 per cent. The increase due to the rise in prices consequently works out at 64 per cent.

The increase in volume is a real contribution to capital formation. The increase in value due to the rise of prices is financially a form of saving, but, being locked up in the stocks of goods, is not available for any other purpose. In reckoning the resources available for capital formation, the profit from the appreciation of stocks is rightly excluded, as it is in the National Income Return.

The Combined Capital Account (Table 6 in the Return for 1946–52) gives the total resources becoming available year by year for capital formation, including depreciation. These resources consist of gross savings, personal and corporate (including tax reserves), *plus* the net provision made by the Government out of revenue for capital purposes.

The provision made by the Government includes, besides the surplus on current account, transfers to capital accounts (such as war damage compensation, refunds of excess profits tax, and, in 1946 and 1947, war gratuities),[1] and the taxes on capital (death duties and special contribution) are deducted. In the subjoined table the receipts from sales of surplus war stores, whether at home or abroad, together with net receipts from war settlements, etc., abroad, are added on to the resources provided by the Government, and the expenditure on strategic stocks is excluded.

TABLE VIII

	1946	1947	1948	1949	1950	1951	1952
Capital Resources provided by Persons & Companies	782	459	738	965	828	816	1,656
provided by additions to Tax Reserves	− 72	212	163	12	126	536	120
provided by Govt. and Local Authorities	− 126	403	747	725	789	579	389
Total	584	1,074	1,648	1,702	1,743	1,931	2,165
Capital Outlay	900	1,160	1,393	1,534	1,674	1,863	2,054
Excess of Resources	− 316	− 86	255	168	69	68	111
Change in Stocks	− 12	+378	+213	+ 65	− 183	+506	− 165
Balance of Payments	− 298	− 443	+ 1	+ 31	+298	− 410	+269
Residual Error	− 6	− 21	+ 41	+ 72	− 46	− 28	+ 7
	− 316	− 86	255	168	69	68	111

[1] See footnote on p. 6.

The excess of capital resources over capital outlay is equal to the sum of the increase in stocks and the favourable balance of payments (with negative sign where appropriate). The 'residual error' is the difference between them attributable to statistical imperfections.[1]

The figures in the table differ from those in Table 6 of the National Income Return for 1946–52, in that the changes and corrections made in the subsequent Balance of Payments White Paper (Cmd. 8976) have been embodied in them. Defence Aid from the United States in 1951 and 1952 is included in the Government's revenue receipts, and therefore in capital resources provided by the Government, as being payment for services rendered.

The shrinkage in capital resources provided by persons and companies in 1947 and again in the two years 1950 and 1951 is partly attributable to the fact that in those years tax had to be paid on exceptionally large profits arising from the appreciation of stocks (£450 million in 1947, £700 million in 1950 and £800 million in 1951). As has been explained above, these profits are locked up in the stocks held, while the tax upon them has to be met from the taxpayers' other resources.

In 1946 the adverse balance of payments corresponded closely with the excess outlay. In 1947 the excess outlay accounted for but little of the adverse balance, and that year and the two following years together saw an increase of stocks by £656 million.

The three years 1950–2 were marked by violent alternations between a depletion of stocks with a favourable balance, and a replenishment of stocks with an adverse balance, the net effect being an excess of resources such as to permit an increase of stocks by £158 million and a net favourable balance of £157 million.

But, in view of the import restrictions enforced in 1949–50 and again in 1951–2, this favourable result cannot be taken as evidence of the attainment of long-term equilibrium.

---

[1] See *National Income Return*, p. 74.

THE CHANGE OF GOVERNMENT AND MONETARY POLICY

The change from a Socialist to a Conservative Government occurred in October 1951 in the midst of the heavy losses of reserves. As an emergency measure, a renewed restriction of imports was inevitable. A great part of the liberalisation of trade with the other members of the O.E.E.C. was abandoned, and imports from them fell from £489 million in the second half of 1951 to £420 million in the first half of 1952 and £318 million in the second half. Imports from all sources fell from £3,496 million in 1951 to £2,927 million in 1952. The index of volume of imports (100 in 1938) fell from 96 to 88.

But import restrictions supplied no lasting solution of the problem. And devaluation had proved an illusion: the adverse terms of trade had heavily reduced the value of expanding exports in terms of imports, and devaluation had not prevented the adverse balance from becoming more menacing than ever within two years. The new Government turned to the long-neglected policy of credit regulation. Bank rate had remained at its traditional minimum of 2 per cent. for nearly twenty years (except for six weeks at 4 per cent. at the outbreak of war in 1939). The rise to $2\frac{1}{2}$ per cent. on the 8th November 1951 had little more than a symbolic value, but the further advance to 4 per cent. on the 11th March 1952 was substantial. With the rise in Bank rate was associated an exhortation to the banks in December 1951 to take direct steps to discourage borrowers. A concerted restriction of credit by the banks was no new departure. Something of the kind had been in operation ever since the war, but had had little practical result. How far the rather more specific guidance given by the Conservative Chancellor of the Exchequer was more effective it is difficult to say.

THE BUDGET POSITION

Throughout the years 1946–52 wages and prices were rising. Up to 1949 they were rising in sympathy with the monetary expansion and rising wages and prices in America. After 1949 the process was accelerated by devaluation. The British wholesale price index (100 in 1938) rose from 172·7 in 1946 to 226·8 in 1949 and 323·3 in 1952. The weekly wage index (100 in June 1947) rose from 97 in 1946 to 109 in 1949 and 130 in 1952. Hence the successive gains from the appreciation of stocks. The gains were not only on the stocks of materials (the prices of which had already reacted from the high levels of 1951 before the end of 1952); they were also on the wholesale and retail stocks of finished goods, the value of which embodied the cost of both materials and wages.

Since the profit from the appreciation of stocks is taxable income, the rise in this profit from £225 million in 1949 to £700 million in 1950 and £800 million in 1951 goes far to explain the expansion of revenue, which enabled the country to meet the increased cost of armaments with relatively little fiscal effort.

The Socialist Government's budget for 1951–2 was prepared without any sense of impending trouble. In previous years a surplus had been provided sufficient to cover the loans to Local Authorities (for housing, etc.) and other disbursements of a capital character, which are not chargeable against revenue (figuring 'below the line' in the Exchequer Account). In the budget of 1951–2 the anticipated surplus was only £39 million, and left capital expenditure estimated at £457 million unprovided for, and therefore to be met by borrowing. Even the surplus of £380 million which was eventually realised failed by some £160 million to cover the capital expenditure actually incurred.

The increases in taxation, however, while estimated to yield £138 million in 1951–2, contained two important proposals which were not expected to make any considerable contribution to the revenue till subsequent years. The

suspension of initial allowances of depreciation was estimated to produce £170 million in a full year, and the increase
in the tax on distributed profits from 30 per cent. to 50 per
cent. was estimated to yield £65 million (net) in a full year
in comparison with only £5 million in 1951–2. The total
yield of the additional taxes in a full year was estimated at
£388 million, being £250 million more than in 1951–2. It
was this prospective burden that occasioned the huge addition of £536 million to tax reserves in the calendar year 1951.
So far as the capital resources of the country were concerned, this large sum not only made good the apparent
inadequacy of the budget surplus, but compensated the
encroachment on private savings caused by the taxation of
the profits from the appreciation of stocks.

The budget of 1952–3 had to provide for increased
armament expenditure, but when allowance was made for
an American contribution of £85 million by way of Defence
Aid, and for a reduction in the provision for strategic
reserves,[1] the increase in the net budget provision for
defence under all heads was only £65 million.

A liberal estimate of the natural growth of revenue held
out the prospect of a surplus of more than £500 million on
the basis of existing taxation. The budget proposals were
important. A reduction of the food subsidies at the rate of
£160 million in a full year, was more than balanced by
concessions in the lower ranges of income tax, and increases
in National Insurance benefits. But important additions to
taxation ensured a net gain to the Exchequer. Among these
was the Excess Profits Levy, estimated to yield in a full
year a net £100 million (after allowing for compensating
adjustments of Profits Tax and Income Tax).

There resulted estimates promising a surplus of £430
million, being a little less than enough to cover capital outlays. But revenue fell short of the estimate by £222 million,

[1] *Strategic Reserves (in £ millions):*

			Estimated	Spent
1951–2	..	..	143	179
1952–3	..	..	53	68
1953–4	..	..	48	—

and expenditure (including a substantial non-recurrent item) exceeded the original budget estimate by £120 million. The surplus was only £88 million and fell short of covering capital disbursements by £436 million.

It must be borne in mind that this out-turn relates to the financial year 1952–3, which includes the first three months of 1953. The corresponding official estimates of national income do not extend beyond the calendar year 1952. The calendar year shows a falling off of the capital resources provided by the Government from £579 million in 1951 to £389 million in 1952, and of the additions to tax reserves from £536 million to £120 million. But this loss of £606 million was more than made up by the increase in savings from £816 million to £1,656 million. There resulted a net increase in the amount of capital resources provided, which, along with the quantitative reduction of £165 million in stocks, made possible the favourable balance of payments of £291 million in 1952.

PRICES AND PROFITS

It is noteworthy that 1952 was the first year since the end of the war that saw no appreciable net increase in the price level of goods held in stock. We have been excluding the profit from the rise of prices of stocks from real capital formation, because it is tied up in the stocks and is not available for any other purpose. For the same reason it should be excluded from disposable profits. The following table shows (in £ millions) the remarkable rise in disposable profits in 1952:

TABLE IX

	1946	1947	1948	1949	1950	1951	1952
Gross Profits	2,591	2,938	3,176	3,323	3,654	4,181	3,896
Stock Appreciation	150	450	325	225	700	800	50
Disposable Gross Profits	2,441	2,488	2,851	3,098	2,954	3,381	3,846

When prices are rising there tends to be some setback in disposable profits. The prudent manufacturer, when he gets an order, provides himself with materials (by a forward purchase, if necessary) at the price he reckoned on when tendering. In the course of a year he makes successive purchases at rising prices, and receives, on completion of an order, a sum calculated to cover his costs in respect of that order and to yield a profit.

But his expenditure on purchases of materials during the whole year will only have been fully recouped when the orders on which he is engaged at the end of the year are completed in the following year. His profits realised in the year do not correspond to his costs disbursed in the year, and the difference is tied up in the goods in stock and in process at the end of the year. A retailer who sells goods at the prices he paid for them, *plus* a conventional margin of profit, is in the same position. Not however a wholesale dealer, who claims a freer hand in pricing his goods, and may be charging full replacement value on the goods he sells at the end of the year.

In the following year the producer or retailer will dispose of the goods he held at the beginning, and will realise the profit on them, and, if prices cease to rise, the profit tied up at the end of the year will be no greater than at the beginning; disposable profits will be the full amount corresponding to the costs disbursed in the year. If prices fall, disposable profits will exceed the profits of the year, and there will be a liquidation of working capital.

A rise of wages in the course of a year has the same effect as a rise in the cost of materials, and, in addition, is likely to encroach on the true profits of the year, unless it is foreseen at the time when a manufacturer quotes his price. But at a time of expanding demand the rise of wages generally lags behind the rise of prices, and profit margins are increased rather than diminished.

It is, therefore, especially the prices of materials that affect the progress of disposable profits. The position is illustrated by the relative price levels of manufactures and materials. There is no general index of British prices of manufactures, but the price index of exports of manufactures will serve. In 1947 the price index of imported materials rose by 28 per cent. above 1946, while the price index of exported manufactures rose by only 17 per cent. Disposable profits in 1947 showed no appreciable increase.

In 1950 the price index of imported materials rose 22 per cent. over 1949 and that of exported manufactures only 4 per cent. And in 1951 the increases over 1950 were 55 per cent. and 18 per cent. respectively. The prices of materials reached a maximum in June 1951 and fell in the second half of the year. The fall continued in 1952, and by May 1953 the rise since 1949 had been reduced to 36 per cent. The prices of exported manufactures on the other hand rose in 1952 to 30 per cent. above the price level of 1949. Margins were by that time not very far below those of 1949. Disposable profits were 24 per cent. higher, or a little less than in proportion to the rise of prices. The relatively low disposable profits in 1950 and 1951 are clearly explained.

There was a fall of about 2 per cent. in the price level of exported manufactures in the latter part of 1952, which was mainly due to textiles, the price index of which dropped from 169 in January 1952 to 147 in June and to 135 in December. It is characteristic of textile products that the cost of raw material accounts for a relatively considerable proportion of the price charged to the consumer. The very high prices of raw cotton and wool reached in the early months of 1951 (two and a half to three times the prices of 1949) had a marked deterrent effect on consumer demand. As the high prices were world-wide, the deterrent effect was world-wide. Everywhere textile industries became depressed.

In the British textile and clothing industries the index of production (100 in 1948) averaged 117 in 1950 and 125 in the first half of 1951. It fell in the second half to $105\frac{1}{2}$, and in August 1952 was only 80. The number of unemployed in these industries rose from 11,100 in June 1951 to 50,200 in December 1951, and 160,700 in May 1952. The numbers employed fell from 1,686,000 in June 1951 to 1,504,000 in June 1952.

Within its limits this was quite a severe setback, but only a part of its effects was felt in 1951, and it did not seriously detract from the generally profitable tendency in industry as a whole in that year. By the end of 1952 recovery in the textile industries was well on its way. That the numbers in the industries, employed and unemployed, had then diminished by 50,000 is an indication of the state of over-employment and the intense demand for labour which then prevailed in industry generally.

If it is true that at the time of the devaluation of 1949 British industry was not suffering from excessive costs, then the rise of 44 per cent. in the sterling value of the dollar would point ultimately to a proportionate rise in the British price level and wage level, and in the British national income. By 1952 the price level of British exports had risen about 30 per cent. since 1949. But it would be wrong to acclaim this as marking two-thirds of the journey towards equilibrium. For the prices of exports contain an element representing the cost of materials, and the index of prices of imported materials had risen more than 50 per cent. The index of weekly wages rose from 109 in 1949 to 134 at the end of 1952 or 23 per cent. Average weekly earnings in manufacturing industries rose from 120s. 10d. in October 1949 to 150s. 10d. in October 1952, or 25 per cent. So long as full employment prevails, the wage level is the best measure of monetary expansion, but even so we should not be justified in concluding that the country has arrived half-way towards correcting the dis-equilibrium set up by devaluation. For there has been a further rise in American wages since 1949. The average hourly earnings in manufacturing industry rose from \$1·40 in 1949 to \$1·715 at the end of 1952. The increase of $22\frac{1}{2}$ per cent. may not be strictly comparable with the increase in Great Britain of 25 per cent. But it is clear that the progress which has been

F

made towards eliminating the inequalities caused by devaluation is but small.

DEVALUATION AND IMPORT PRICES

The policy of devaluation was the outcome of a misconception as to the causes of the adverse balance of payments. But it did have some beneficial effects. Devaluation raises the prices of imports in terms of the money unit, and so diminishes demand for the imported goods. The deterrent effect on imports may improve the balance of payments even though, owing to the fall of export prices in foreign money units, the expansion of exports fails to yield any net increase in proceeds. The deterrent effect on imports is itself likely to be only temporary, for it depends on the disparity between the prices of imports and the national income, that is to say, the flow of purchasing power in terms of the national money unit. The national income tends to expand in proportion to the devaluation. The principal factor in such expansion is the wage level; a wide discrepancy between wages and profits is sure to correct itself.

The appeal of the Government in 1949 for a standstill of wages was no doubt primarily actuated by the desire to keep down costs in the export industries. But it also had a bearing upon the deterrent effect of high sterling prices on the demand for imports.

In the circumstances of Great Britain in 1949 controls had gone far to exclude non-essential imports, and the imports which were permitted could not be very responsive to a rise of price. But, wherever foreign prices reflected the depreciation of sterling, the limitation of imports became less dependent on quantitative restriction, and the prospect of restoring free markets and relying on the deterrent effect of high prices upon consumption was improved. For example, the liberalisation of trade with Western Europe was facilitated, though in the event liberalisation was found to have gone too far.

Devaluation spread to the whole Sterling Area (except Pakistan), and the rise in the sterling value of dollar goods may be assumed to have helped materially towards the reduction of dollar imports into the overseas Sterling Area in 1950. In 1951 and the first half of 1952 the swollen proceeds of their exports of primary products led to correspondingly high imports, but the drop of their dollar imports from $830 million in the first half of 1952 to $530 million in the second half may be attributed to high prices reckoned in sterling as well as to quantitative restrictions.

DEVALUATION AND REDUNDANT MONEY

Devaluation also contributed to the solution of the problem of redundant money. In 1949 net bank deposits averaged £5,772 million and currency in the hands of the public £1,248 million, making the supply of money £7,020 million. In 1952 net bank deposits averaged £5,857 million and currency £1,382 million, so that the supply of money was £7,239 million and had increased only 3 per cent. (variations in intermediate years having been small). The flow of money, as measured by gross national product, had risen from £10,926 million in 1949 to £13,653 million in 1952, or 25 per cent. In 1938 the stock of money, £2,663 million, amounted to the value of about six months' production, so that the corresponding amount for 1952 would be £6,826 million. That calculation would make the excess only some £400 million. But it is not to be concluded that the excess supply of money has become negligible. The year 1938, being one of depression and stagnation of cash balances, was not typical (above, p. 16). Still the excess supply of money may fairly be supposed to be substantially less than the total of bank advances, which in 1952 averaged £1,838 million. It had become possible by restricting advances to eliminate what was left of the redundant money. Not quite, perhaps. It is not practicable to reduce bank advances to nothing, and any considerable reduction takes time.

But the effects of devaluation had not been exhausted. The rise of British prices and wages had still a long way to go before they could be once more in equilibrium with foreign money units, and a stage would be reached in the rise at which there would actually be a need for an expansion of the money supply to sustain the enlarged flow of money.

Up to now the equilibrium point has been receding, because American prices and wages have been rising. The rise might be reversed, and the equilibrium point brought nearer. But a substantial monetary contraction in America is hardly a contingency to be taken into account. The Employment Act of 1947 establishes full employment as a statutory object of policy. American ideas, it may be said, as to the means by which full employment is to be maintained, are not very clear. But so long as the view is generally accepted that dear money tends to cause a decline of activity and a diminution of employment, a violent monetary contraction on the model of the years 1929–32 is not likely to occur.

A recession, it is true, may be started by other causes than a monetary contraction. The revival in American industry, which brought down the number of unemployed from 12,830,000 in 1933 to 7,700,000 in 1937, was abruptly stopped by the rise of wages which increased average hourly earnings from 55·6 cents in 1936 to 62·4 cents in 1937, and the number of unemployed rose in 1938 to 10,390,000. It is perhaps significant that in 1953 hourly earnings have been rising from 171·5 cents in December 1952 to 177 cents in June 1953 in spite of a slight setback to activity. But a rise of wages will only cause a recession if there is some impediment, whether institutional or psychological, to a corresponding expansion of the flow of money. A time may come when the antipathy to dear money is outweighed by misgiving as to the outcome of an indefinitely continuing rise of prices and wages, but there seems to be no prospect of such a change of attitude in the near future. At the present time (January 1954) there is actually a pause in the rising process, but it is probably no more than a pause. While it lasts, it entirely removes any prospect of measures of credit restriction, and in the absence of such measures there will be no serious recession.

We may assume, therefore, that, if the existing rate of exchange of $2·80 to £1 remains unchanged, the inflationary tendency which has been felt in Great Britain since 1949 will continue. Wages and prices will rise, and the Gross National Product expressed in monetary units will increase.

American hourly earnings at 177 cents have now risen 26 per cent. since 1949. Are we to infer that British wages must rise up to a limit at which they have made a relative gain of 44 per cent. upon this rise? A rise of 44 per cent. superimposed on a rise of 26 per cent. would make a rise of 80 per cent. above the level of 1949.

BRITISH AND AMERICAN PRODUCTIVITY

Allowance must be made for structural changes. British Industry may fail to keep pace with American in improvement of productivity. Productivity per man-hour is much higher in American industry than in British. As to the magnitude of the disparity and its causes, how far it is attributable to the superior natural resources of the United States, how far to deeper capitalisation and mechanisation, how far to organisation and management, how far to greater zeal and efficiency of labour, these are questions into which I am not prepared to enter. The disparity calls for a rate of exchange which makes American wages higher than British in terms of money.

In 1938 average hourly earnings in manufacturing in the United States were 62·7 cents, in Great Britain 13d. At the average rate of exchange of the year, $4·89 to £1, the latter rate was equivalent to 26½ cents. American hourly earnings were therefore 2·36 times British. In 1949 American hourly earnings were 140 cents, while British at 32·3d. were equivalent, at the pre-devaluation rate of exchange, 4·03, to 54 cents. The proportion had thus grown to 2·59 to 1. Devaluation raised it to 3·73 to 1.

Is there any ground for supposing that the disparity in productivity is growing greater?

The available statistical evidence relating to manufacturing and mining, in both countries, suggests that the difference is not important, as the following table shows:

TABLE X

	Index of Industrial Production	Thousands Employed	Index of Production per head
United Kingdom			
1948 ...	100	9,013	100·0
1949 ...	106	9,174	104·1
1950 ...	114	9,362	109·7
1951 ...	117	9,592	109·9
1952 ...	114	9,501	108·1
United States			
1948 ...	192	16,267	100·0
1949 ...	176	15,078	98·9
1950 ...	200	15,788	107·3
1951 ...	220	16,851	110·6
1952 ...	219	16,781	110·6

Too much reliance should not be placed on the statistics of either country, but at any rate it is safe to say that any loss of relative productivity would not be such as materially to affect the limits of the monetary expansion to which Great Britain has been committed by devaluation.

The foregoing comparison takes no account of the big increase in American productivity between 1938 and 1948, when the index of manufacturing production rose from 87 to 198, and the numbers employed only from 9,253,000 to 15,286,000, indicating an increase in productivity per head of 38 per cent., whereas in the same period in Great Britain there seems to have been no increase at all. Allowance must be made, however, for the exceptional conditions of the year 1938 in American industry. Depression has a very marked effect on the current productivity per head in mass-producing industries, and productivity per head in the United States suffered heavily in the nineteen-thirties. It was actually 9 per cent. less in 1938 than in 1929.

EXPORTING POWER

But the problem of the balance of payments is not one exclusively of productivity. Productivity has to be considered in relation to exporting power, and British exporting power has to be reckoned mainly in terms of manufactured goods. To develop and maintain an export trade, it is essential that costs be competitive, but it is no less essential that the products offered suit the purchasers, not only that they are such as to meet the purchasers' needs and purposes, but that they conform to custom, taste and fashion. In the past British exporters have learnt to comply with these requirements, and they have had in the present century to pit their skill and experience against those of rival exporters, especially German, Japanese and American.

During the war the greater part of their export trade was in abeyance. But so was that of their principal rivals, except the United States. For some years after the end of the war neither Germany nor Japan was an effective competitor in British export markets. The export drive rapidly raised British exports from 31 per cent. of their pre-war volume in 1944 to 174 per cent. in 1950 and 176 in 1951. The decline in 1952 to 165 per cent. was due rather to the general decline of demand in the world for textile products than to growing competition in all markets.

But growing competition has to be faced. It is possible that the technical progress and increased mechanisation of the present century have diminished the importance of custom, fashion and taste in guiding consumers' preferences. Products which are judged by their mechanical effectiveness play an increased part in international trade, also innovations which offer themselves on their merits with no tradition behind them, such as refrigerators, television sets or washing machines. Newcomers to trade, with nothing but their own technical competence to recommend them, therefore have better opportunities than formerly, so that industrialisation has come more within the reach of under-developed countries.

Undoubtedly in the future British producers for export will have to meet a high pressure of competition. Costs not too high will be a necessary but not a sufficient condition of success; quality of product will be as fundamental. And that does not always mean high quality; the cost of supplying a better quality than the consumer or user wants may be sheer waste. For Great Britain, with its dependence on indispensable imports, much depends on the success of exporters in taking opportunities and overcoming difficulties. Of their prospects I offer no opinion. But as we have seen, the reduction of costs which devaluation has brought about can be no more than a limited remedy for shortcomings in other directions, and may be no remedy at all.

Whatever the scale of the future export trade of the country, importing power must somehow conform to exporting power. An adverse balance cannot continue indefinitely. In other words, the country cannot go on spending in excess of its income and therefore in excess of its output.

Chapter Four

CREDIT POLICY

THE ENGLISH CREDIT SYSTEM

WE have seen (above, p. 40) that excess spending is only possible so far as the spenders possess or can procure money in excess of what they receive by way of income, and that monetary policy can prevent the excess spending by depriving the would-be spenders of this excess money. The banks are the source of money, and they have the power to cut off the supply of it. Their liabilities (deposits and notes) in which the supply of money consists, are backed by their assets, and they can reduce their liabilities by reducing their assets.

The assets of the banks are composed partly of money lent for short periods, partly of investments which are chiefly Government securities due for repayment within moderate periods of years. A commercial bank is concerned with its own liquidity, not with monetary policy. Liquidity consists for it in being able to provide its depositors with whatever currency they need, and to meet its liabilities in clearing accounts with other banks. Currency is provided by the Bank of England, and deposits at the Bank of England are the medium in which clearing liabilities are paid. The credit system is therefore centralised in the Bank of England. The Bank of England, by lending or by acquiring securities, creates currency, or deposits equivalent to currency. The deposits form the cash reserves of the other banks, upon the maintenance of which their liquidity depends.

It is a long-standing tradition that the English banks do

not sell bills. The discount market buys bills, and procures funds for the purpose by borrowing at call from the banks. When a bank needs cash it can call up money from the discount market, and it is the discount houses, not the bank, that actually sell bills. If the proceeds of maturing bills in their hands suffice to provide the banks' calls, they do not need to sell. If they do sell, to whom do they sell? In the first instance to one another, but if on balance there is a need of cash, they sell to the Bank of England. That is the traditional procedure, but it has been in part superseded since the banks came to hold large sums in Treasury bills, for a bank can quickly replenish its cash by simply abstaining from the purchase of new bills to replace maturing Treasury bills in its possession.

Bank rate used to mean the rate of discount at which the Bank of England would buy the best commercial bills from the discount market. But nowadays it is rather the rate at which the Bank is willing to buy Treasury bills which governs the market.

Commercial bills have to a great extent been superseded by bank advances, as the method of short-term financing, so that the market rate of discount has become relatively unimportant as a factor in the British credit system. But the practice is to base the rates charged for loans and overdrafts on Bank rate, so that a rise or fall of Bank rate is in general accompanied by an equal rise or fall in the rates charged by the banks to borrowing customers. It is by determining the rates paid for short-term borrowing throughout the community that the Bank of England regulates credit, and through credit the supply of money.

This dependence of the rates charged on bank advances upon Bank rate is not a mere convention. For to a bank advances to customers are an alternative to Treasury bills as a short-term investment, and the Treasury bill rate ultimately depends on the rate at which the Bank of England would buy them in default of adequate applications for them from the banks and other tenderers. The Bank of

England's rate is, of course, closely related to Bank rate.

When Bank rate was reduced on the 17th September 1953 from 4 to $3\frac{1}{2}$ per cent., the rate at which the Bank would lend on the security of Treasury bills[1] remained unchanged at $3\frac{1}{2}$ per cent. Nevertheless the customary relation between Bank rate and the rates on overdrafts and loans was observed, and the market rate of discount on commercial bills fell with these latter.

INFLUENCE OF BANK RATE ON BORROWING

The efficacy of Bank rate as an instrument of monetary policy depends on the response of intending borrowers to an increase or decrease of the rates charged to them, that is to say, on the extent to which they will actually decrease or increase the amounts they borrow. Their response evidently depends on the purposes for which they borrow.

For a genuinely temporary loan, say, for three months, the charge for interest, except at a high rate, is only a small fraction of the capital sum. Where the borrower is a consumer, who wants to anticipate future income for present expenditure, his grounds for doing so, if they are sufficiently urgent for him to contemplate borrowing at all, are unlikely to be outweighed by the charge for interest. But that kind of borrowing is not likely to be a considerable part of the whole.

A private individual is more likely to borrow from his bank in his capacity as investor than in his capacity as consumer. He will borrow in anticipation of future savings to take a favourable opportunity of acquiring shares or property, or to avoid selling in an unfavourable market. There is an important class of short-term borrowers, which includes traders as well as private investors, who need funds for capital purposes in anticipation of the receipt of capital sums, whether from future savings, from sales of capital

---

[1] Not the same as the rate at which the Bank would *buy* Treasury bills, if there were insufficient demand for them.

assets, or from flotations in the investment market. Where the money is required for some considerable capital enterprise, the interest on temporary loans cannot count for much in estimates of its long-range financial result. But if the rate becomes very high and especially if the high rate is reflected in the level of prices of securities in the investment market, the enterprise may be postponed in the hope that conditions may shortly improve.

The most usual occasion for temporary borrowing is for the purchase of goods to replenish a trader's stocks, whether a manufacturer's stock of materials, or a wholesale or retail dealer's stock of goods destined for sale. The amount of goods to be held in stock is a matter of convenience. It must always be kept up to a certain minimum, necessary for carrying on the trader's business (of manufacturing or of selling) without danger of interruption. But it is usually convenient to hold stocks far above the essential minimum. It is an advantage and an economy to handle relatively large consignments of goods for stock; and a trader will often want to take opportunities of buying goods specially suitable to his business on advantageous terms. The trader does not want to be hampered in his purchases by want of ready cash. Yet his cash has to be provided as part of his capital resources, and it may be difficult, especially in a growing business, to set apart a sufficient margin. If he is short of cash, however, he need not stint his business, for the purchase of goods destined for sale is the most eligible purpose for which a banker may lend. (Goods destined for sale include materials to be embodied in finished products destined for sale.) It is for the banker to decide on what terms he will lend, and for the trader to choose whether it is worth while to borrow, or whether it is better to avoid the charges on a bank advance at the cost of the inconvenience of limiting his purchases. Obviously he will be unwilling to reduce his stock below the minimum necessary for carrying on his business without interruption. But there is sure to be a wide margin between the stock which he finds it convenient to hold and this bare minimum. Indeed, he would probably take care not to be dependent on bank advances for carrying the bare minimum. Prudence would require him to provide that essential need from his own capital resources, so that he could reduce his short-term borrowing to nothing without suffering serious embarrassment.

The short-term borrowing of traders for the purchase of goods, being so easily reduced, is very sensitive to the rate of interest charged. Even when the immediate purpose of the borrowing is something other than the purchase of goods for stock, when for example it is some expenditure on renewals or extensions of plant, buildings or equipment, it is still the case that the readiest way by which the trader can reduce his borrowing is by letting down his stocks, that is, by restricting his purchases for stock below the current amount of his sales.

The first step to be taken by a trader who wants to reduce his short-term indebtedness will be to diminish the orders he gives for goods to replace those he sells. If he is buying from another dealer (for example, a retailer buying from a wholesaler) the latter will in turn give diminished orders to replace his sales (still more diminished if he, like the other, wants to reduce his short-term indebtedness). Thus the whole effect of this move to reduce indebtedness by reducing the amount of stocks held is concentrated in the diminution of orders given to producers. That is how a rise in Bank rate reacts so directly on industrial activity. The first impact, however, is on the amount of new orders, and, when there is an accumulation of unexecuted orders, there is an interval for these orders to be worked through, before any visible decline of activity occurs.

The relevance of Bank rate policy to the present situation of Great Britain will now be obvious. Bank rate is not merely the instrument for putting a check to excess spending by restricting the supply of money; it accomplishes this end by causing a decline in orders to producers, and so can directly relieve that congestion of orders and over-employment from which British industry is suffering.

It is the order given to the producer that starts money moving, and is the occasion for the creation of fresh money if the producer's cash balance is insufficient. The producer himself, if he has to borrow, feels the influence of a higher charge for interest on bank advances, but he will not be deterred on that account from accepting the order. He will no doubt look more closely at his stocks of materials and intermediate products, and may give diminished orders to the producers of these, but he will, at all events, see to it that he has the cash to pay the necessary expenses of production, and it is this cash which moves, and which generates incomes. When the producer completes an order and receives payment on delivery of the goods, his cash is replenished, and so much of his bank advances can be repaid.

It is at that stage that the trader who gave the order must produce cash, and may have to borrow. If he is to be influenced by the rate of interest he has to pay, it must be at the time when he gives the order and becomes committed to payment, and when it is the prospective rate at the time of completion of the order that he must reckon on.

A rise in the rate of interest on bank advances is felt by the trader as an increase in the cost of holding so much of his existing stocks as he is financing by borrowing. That is an immediate additional burden, which may be gradually relieved by sales from stock, so far as these are not offset by pending deliveries of goods in compliance with orders to which the trader is already committed. If he now restricts orders for the purpose of saving interest, he must be assuming the continuance of the high rate over the time at which the orders will be completed. And he will in general expect it to continue unless he can point to specific circumstances warranting a contrary view.

The effect of a rise of Bank rate on orders to producers is therefore immediate, while its effect on the supply of money and on the flow of money only follows after the reduction of orders begins to be reflected in diminished productive activity. The effect on the balance of payments becomes visible only when pre-existing orders for imported goods have been worked through, and the time comes for delivery of goods under the diminished orders.

THE RISE OF BANK RATE IN 1952

The 4 per cent. Bank rate which came into operation in March 1952 cannot be reckoned high. At that date the long-term rate of interest (as measured by the yield of $3\frac{1}{2}$ per cent. War Loan) was about $4\frac{1}{2}$ per cent., and had been at 4 per cent. or more since the preceding summer. The long-term rate of interest tends to supply the norm by reference to which both borrowers and lenders reckon the short-term rate to be high or low.

Formerly the convention which related the rate of interest on bank loans and overdrafts to Bank rate, was subject to the limitation that the former rate should not fall below a minimum of 5 per cent. If the conventional rate was 1 per cent above Bank rate, the minimum would lead to any variation of Bank rate below 4 per cent. being disregarded. The minimum had never been fully operative at times of very low Bank rate: it was freely broken into in favour of big and powerful borrowers, and of those who offered gilt-edged collateral security. A rise of Bank rate from 2 to 4 per cent. (as occurred between October 1951 and March 1952) would therefore affect these classes of borrowers. And in the long period of cheap money preceding the outbreak of war in 1939, the traditional minimum rate for overdrafts dropped into abeyance, and few trade borrowers paid more than $3\frac{1}{2}$ per cent. The rise of Bank rate in 1952 therefore had a very real and material effect upon borrowers.

It was accompanied in December 1951 by the notification to bankers, referred to above (p. 59), enjoining them to restrict their advances to customers. The notification was intended to reinforce the dear money policy. How far did it do so? The trader, considering what orders to give to producers for the replenishment of stocks, takes into account the rate of interest he may be charged if he has to borrow to pay for the goods. But he will not take into account the possibility of his banker actually refusing to lend, unless the banker has warned him beforehand that he will not lend. Nor is it practically possible for the banker to refuse to lend to a customer for the unexceptionable purpose of buying goods either for sale or for use in manufacturing in the course of his business, unless he has given a prior warning. If the warning were given, the customer would take care to restrict his orders within the amount he could count on being able to pay for. The warning need not be the prelude to an absolute refusal to lend. The banker may agree to lend but only up to a limit of amount. Thus the severity of the restriction of credit may be graduated. But it is difficult to find any formula to express the degree of restriction which a given credit policy would require. Direct restriction or rationing of credit is much less flexible and adaptable than the method of varying Bank rate. How far it has helped towards the working of the monetary policy adopted since the change of Government in 1951 it would be difficult to estimate.

Bank advances had risen under the influence of cheap money from £759 million at the end of hostilities in 1945, to £1,897 million in October 1951. For the next six months the total continued to increase, and it reached £1,953 million in April 1952. Thereafter it fell to £1,749 million at the end of the year. The further fall in 1953 (to £1,676 million in November) has been slower.

THE DEFICIT

Something had been accomplished, but bank advances did not tell the whole story. We saw above (p. 60) that revenue provided by the budget of 1951-2 failed by £160 million to cover the capital outlays charged to the Exchequer, and that the deficiency in the financial year 1952-3 rose to £436 million. This deficiency was financed through the creation of credit by the banks. The Clearing Banks' holdings of Treasury bills, Treasury deposit receipts and Investments rose from £2,858 million at the end of December 1951 to £3,396 million at the end of December 1952. Seasonal influences are apt to distort the end of the year figures. But those for March, when Treasury bills reach a seasonal minimum, record the same tendency, a rise from £2,613 million in March 1952 to £3,077 million in March 1953. At the same time the active note issue of the Bank of England (backed by Government securities) rose from £1,380 million in March 1952 to £1,481 million in March 1953.

Since the change of Government in 1951, therefore, there has been fresh inflation more than sufficient to nullify the contractive effects of the new monetary policy. Moreover, the budget for 1953-4 provides a surplus of only £109 million, leaving capital outlays estimated at £549 million uncovered. The deficiency need not all be financed by inflationary methods: it might be met by the flotation in the investment market of loans of the type which investors would take. The serial stocks, maturing in one, two and three years, which were issued in November 1951, November 1952 and November 1953, appeal primarily to banks, and to overseas holders of sterling, who would otherwise take Treasury bills. Even when acquired by business concerns for investment of balance sheet reserves, they are practically the equivalent of ready cash, destined for early spending.

What is wanted is the kind of security that suits the long-term investor, either a funded stock repayable only at the option of the Government, or a long-dated stock repayable at a distant date (twenty years or more). It would compete in the investment market with other flotations for the

G

permanent placing of the investors' savings. Money raised by it would be withdrawn from the resources available in the market for capital outlay other than that of the Government. That is the essential condition of its disinflationary effect.

The 3 per cent. 10-year stock put into issue in October 1953 does not fully meet the case. It is not exclusively a banker's security, for it is very suitable for the investment of a trader's undistributed profits or accumulating depreciation allowance, if the money will have to be spent and the security realised in the course of a few years. But the yield is unattractive to an investor who is seeking a permanent income and does not expect to require a capital sum in the near future.

A Flexible Bank Rate

When Bank rate was reduced from 4 to $3\frac{1}{2}$ per cent. on the 17th September, whispers were heard that the purpose was to prepare a favourable market for pending issues of Government securities and of denationalised steel shares. A reduction actuated by such a purpose however could not be expected to last long, and the relatively considerable effect on the prices of Government securities implied that the market was seeing in it a more substantial change of policy.

But surely the time has not come for any relaxation of credit. The reduction of Bank rate was accompanied by an intimation that the intention was to prepare the way for a more flexible Bank rate. That would be all to the good. A special virtue of Bank rate is its prompt adaptability to any change in circumstances.

In the management of credit prompt action is called for in consequence of the inherent instability of credit: any movement of expansion or contraction, unless quickly checked, tends to set up a vicious circle by which the movement exaggerates itself. An incipient movement can be checked by a moderate rise or fall of Bank rate, but the high or low rate ought not to be continued after it has done its work.

It is possible that the 4 per cent. Bank rate imposed in March 1952 was not high enough; the fact that it was accompanied by exhortations to the banks not to lend too freely implies that it was not even supposed to be. Its continuance unchanged for eighteen months was a departure from former Bank rate practice. A revival of the policy of flexibility would be highly desirable, though the circumstances of September 1953 were hardly such as to warrant the initiation of that policy by a reduction.

SPENDING AND CAPITAL FORMATION

Inflation means spending in excess of income. If saving is the excess of income over consumption, and spending other than on consumption is spending on capital formation, then spending in excess of income means spending on capital formation in excess of saving. The table of Capital Resources (above, p. 57) shows that the excess has to be met from stocks and from excess imports. The maintenance of stocks at a level acceptable to the traders who hold them is a legitimate part of capital formation. When excess spending is met from stocks, that is only a temporary expedient; even if stocks were previously redundant, continued excess spending will eventually reduce them below normal. An excess of imports, which has to be paid for out of monetary reserves, is likewise a temporary expedient. If it is paid for by loans or grants from abroad, it is no longer an excess. The grants or loans are a means of settling the balance, and extinguishing the excess, though they may be what Professor Meade calls Accommodating Payments, which have been provided expressly to cover the balance. Such payments supplement drafts upon the monetary reserves, but they cannot be continued for ever.

Monetary policy stops excess spending by cutting short the supply of money. In particular cases excess spending may be on consumption. The spendthrift may be dissipating his inheritance, and, since the war subjected the highest incomes to crippling taxation, it has been only too common for the wealthy man to maintain so much as he can of his former manner of living by drawing on his capital. But more usually prudence requires spending in excess of income to be on some valuable asset: the consumer acquires investments or property of permanent value, the trader spends on capital equipment, or on stocks of goods. If excess spending is prevented, it will be chiefly these forms of accumulation that will be diminished.

Can the country afford to let its rate of capital accumulation fall off? With given defence expenditure a stop to excess spending must have that effect unless it causes a decrease of consumption. The controls which inflicted austerity were designed to safeguard accumulation. Taxation serves the same purpose, unless direct taxation is pushed so far as to encroach on saving. When taxation fails to cover the charges on the Exchequer for capital outlay, and, to avoid inflation, the money for meeting the deficiency is raised from the resources of the investment market, the money available for other capital outlay is reduced, but that means no more than that capital outlay is kept within the limits imposed by saving.

But did not Keynes maintain that saving is determined by 'investment' (i.e. capital formation), not investment by saving? Not unconditionally. His contention presupposed that the productive resources of the community were *under-employed*, so that any new demand for the production of capital equipment could bring unemployed productive power into activity without diminishing the production already at work, and would therefore generate additional incomes. When there is full employment, his argument ceases to apply.

When Bank rate is put up, and bank advances are discouraged, capital formation is diminished. But the diminution is mainly (perhaps entirely) in the formation of working capital, the accumulation of stocks of goods. When stocks held are well above the minimum required for carrying on the traders' business of producing and selling, the diminution does not affect their business. In the first instance it is the orders for the replenishment of stocks that fall off. If there is a congestion of orders, there is no actual falling-off of production or of employment till pending orders have been worked through. At that stage the reduction in orders given, which occurred when the credit stringency started, begins to take effect in reduced deliveries. If the credit stringency is persisted in, and traders continue trying to reduce their borrowing by reducing their stocks, the diminished orders will then be reflected in a decline of productive activity and of employment. But if the excess orders, which have been causing the adverse balance of payments, have been eliminated, the credit stringency has done its work and can be discontinued, or at any rate abated. Thereafter credit policy should be so adjusted that the existing level of stocks is acceptable to the traders who hold them, so that the orders given to producers are neither more nor less than enough to replace sales (subject to the need for a long-range growth of stocks in proportion to the production of a progressive community).

The excess spending which causes an adverse balance of payments may thus take the form of spending on an enlargement of stocks, which can be checked by credit control, provided a sufficient proportion of the stocks is held with borrowed money, and provided also that the amount of stocks held is not too near the minimum. A trader becomes extremely resistant to pressure if a curtailment of his borrowing means a reduction of his stocks below the essential level with which he can carry on his business without interruption and consequent loss.

ACTIVE ACCUMULATION

If the purchase of goods for stock is part of capital formation, and is a form of spending which has to be taken into account in reckoning the amount of excess spending, then our assumption that excess spending is met from stocks needs revision. To say that the addition to stocks is met from stocks is nonsense.

The increase or decrease in the aggregate of traders' stocks is the resultant, on the one side, of the traders' action in purchasing or ordering goods, and, on the other, of the action of the consumers and users of the goods to whom the traders sell. A trader's purchases are primarily to replace his sales, but he may think an increase or a decrease in his stock desirable, and may accordingly order either more or less than the equivalent of the amount sold. When traders' stocks, on the whole, are below the level which the traders think desirable, their purchases in excess of sales are directed to capital formation. But their sales depend on the spending power of the consumers and users, and the traders' orders to producers cause an enlargement of the producers' incomes (through increased activity or higher prices) and therefore of their spending power. The action taken by the traders to increase their stocks thus results in an increase in their sales, which partially defeats their object. (This is one aspect of the vicious circle which gives rise to the inherent instability of credit.)

Excess spending is the excess of spending as a whole over incomes as a whole. Spending is composed of consumption, *plus* Government spending, *plus* the formation of capital. And the formation of capital is composed of capital outlay *plus* what may be called 'active accumulation' of stocks, that is to say, so much of traders' purchases for stock as is *intended* to add to the total of stocks. Active accumulation of stocks may be a negative quantity, for traders may find their existing stocks excessive, and may reduce their orders for replenishment below the equivalent of their sales.

The traders' efforts to increase their stocks come into conflict with their own action in increasing their orders to producers, and generating incomes which become the source of a new demand on stocks. Stocks however can be replenished not only from home production, but from imported supplies. And the home production, if it is diverted from export markets, does not generate additional incomes. An adverse balance of payments provides a resource for replenishing stocks without generating additional demand. Given untrammelled access to this resource, an increase in stocks might be identified with active accumulation and included in the total of spending.

In the post-war years this identification is not possible. Import restrictions interfered with imported supplies; the export drive withheld exportable goods from the home market; and price controls exposed producers to an inflated demand at home.

The American and Canadian loans in 1947 and Marshall Aid, combined with a big budget surplus, in 1948, provided the resources for accumulating stocks in those years. As prices and wages were rising in sympathy with the inflationary process in America, the restrictive effect of price controls on accumulation was diminished. The increase in the volume of stocks (about 15 per cent.) was a partial relief of the acute shortage consequent on war conditions.

Progress towards relief of the shortage was summarily interrupted by the import restrictions imposed in July 1949, and there was an actual net decrease of stocks in 1950. The liberalisation of trade with Western Europe and other measures of relaxation opened the way to an increase of stocks in 1951 by £1,306 million, of which £506 million represented the increase in quantity. Whether at that moment the stocks held, as a whole, had reached an acceptable level, we have no means of telling. In 1952 import restrictions were once again intensified. But the credit policy embodied in the rise of Bank rate to 4 per cent. was a new factor. Credit restriction, by making traders less willing to hold stocks of goods with borrowed money, reduces the acceptable level of stocks. It is possible, therefore, that their stocks may have still been below the acceptable level at the end of 1951, and yet above it in 1952, and that the decrease of stocks in 1952 by £115 million (by £165 million in quantity) may have been the outcome of a deliberate intention on traders' part of holding lower stocks. Savings were at a high level in 1952, their increase since 1950 having been more than sufficient to make up for the fall of £400 million in capital resources provided by the Government.

Active accumulation of stocks, being defined in terms of the traders' desires and intentions, eludes statistical measurement. A statistical comparison of capital resources with capital outlay and the balance of payments accounts for the actual change in stocks of goods. In interpreting this change, we must make the best assumption we can as to the level of stocks which would be acceptable.

When we said (above, p. 83) that the meeting of excess spending from stocks is only a temporary expedient because it will eventually reduce stocks below normal, we gave no explanation of what is 'normal'. As soon as stocks are reduced below what is 'acceptable', active accumulation is set up to restore them, and active accumulation will obtain resources, if permitted, from an excess of imports. If import restrictions are imposed, and an export drive is maintained, active accumulation comes into direct competition with other forms of spending, that is to say, consumption, capital outlay and Government expenditure (including defence). If these other forms of spending continue unabated, the excess goes on being met from stocks, and the pressure towards active accumulation becomes so much the greater.

Tighter credit, by lowering the acceptable level of stocks, diminishes or reverses active accumulation, and so makes room for more spending under other heads. When excess spending is met from stocks, the reduction of stocks no longer conflicts with traders' desires, but accords with them. It is a move towards equilibrium.

THE ACCEPTABLE LEVEL OF STOCKS

Suppose, for example, that the Government is incurring a deficit (caused, perhaps, by defence expenditure) at the rate of £20 million a month, and that the resulting excess spending is being met from stocks. Over a short period the diminution of stocks would be negligible in comparison with stocks of the order of £7,000 million. But the orders given by traders for the replenishment of their stocks will be determined by the actual state of the stocks, and in the first month may be presumed to be £20 million greater. If full employment prevails, the additional orders fail to bring about any additional output; the total of outstanding orders grows by £20 million every month. In the course of seven months it will have grown by £140 million, and stocks will be short of the acceptable level by 2 per cent. Under the pressure of an extra £140 million of orders, producers, who were already fully employed, would raise their prices; partly because price has to be remunerative to the least efficient producers; partly because premiums are asked for early delivery; partly because producers are tempted to charge what the market will bear. The producers also seek to take advantage of the high demand by extending output; they need more labour, and the workpeople take the opportunity to press demands for higher wages. At the same time, wholesale and retail dealers, experiencing delay in replenishing their stocks, defend them by charging prices above replacement value. There is a general rise of prices and wages, and the supply of money expands automatically in proportion, for the borrowers need more in proportion to the rise in the prices or costs which they have to pay. The result, in a word, is inflation.

Suppose now that the short-term rate of interest is raised, and that traders become less willing to hold stocks with borrowed money, so that the acceptable level of stocks is reduced by, say, 10 per cent. from £7,000 million to £6,300 million. We have been assuming that stocks have been reduced by £140 million to £6,860 million, but the latter figure is £560 million above the new acceptable level.

Traders, therefore, begin to restrict their purchases and orders. Far from raising prices to check consumer demand, they will be more inclined to make price concessions in order to sell off goods and reduce indebtedness. The pressure on productive capacity is relieved, producers cease to raise their prices, the demand for labour falls off and the ground is no longer favourable to a rise of wages.

So long as the producers are working through the accumulation of £140 million of outstanding orders, there is no decline in production, and the reduction in stocks is confined to the £20 million a month corresponding to the Government's excess spending. But the monthly output of stock-held products (manufactures and agricultural and mineral products) is about £500 million, so that the total orders received by producers would average approximately that amount, and a curtailment by £140 million could take effect very quickly. A stage would soon be reached at which a further curtailment of orders is needed to bring down stocks to the acceptable level, and this further curtailment will mean an actual decline in productive activity and an under-employment of industry. A policy of full employment would then demand a relaxation of credit so calculated as to raise the acceptable level of stocks to equality with the actual level. Orders to producers would once more equal sales from stocks, and thereupon the gradual depletion of stocks by £20 million a month would start again. It would start, however, with higher interest charges and a lower acceptable level of stocks and a lower actual level than before. As before, after an interval, inflationary symptoms would appear, dearer money would be imposed, and, on the threat of unemployment, would be relaxed.

The acceptable level of stocks has to be repeatedly lowered lest the decline in the actual level caused by the Government's excess spending give rise to inflation. The alternations of tight and loose credit, which we have been supposing, are a consequence of the assumption that action will not be taken unless the tendency to inflation or to unemployment becomes palpable and imminent. We might have assumed instead that the authorities in charge of credit policy, taking a long view, do not wait for symptoms of imminent inflation, but raise the short-term rate of interest step by step, always keeping it just short of the limit at which unemployment would appear.

In practice, of course, neither assumption is likely to be realised. Nor is inflationary expenditure by the Government incurred at an unvarying monthly rate. If credit policy is relied on to prevent inflation, the application of dear money to counteract excess spending by the Government is likely to be by tentative and irregular steps.

But underlying all the various possible assumptions is the progressively restrictive credit policy. Any departure in the direction of credit relaxation raises the acceptable level of stocks and sets up active accumulation with inflationary effect. The inflationary effect of Government spending arises from the resulting depletion of stocks, and has to be counteracted by measures which reduce the acceptable level. But the reduction of the acceptable level of stocks cannot go on for ever. No credit measures can reduce the acceptable level below the limit at which a shortage of stocks threatens to interrupt a trader's business. And, with the structure of British bank assets as it is at the present time, the proportion of stocks carried with borrowed money appears to be hardly one-sixth. Bank advances in Great Britain in February 1953 (including Scotland as well as the English Clearing Banks) amounted to £1,868 million, of which only about £1,200 million appear to have been to traders in stock-held goods. Nothing that a reduction of advances could do would bring down stocks anywhere near the minimum.

The efficacy, therefore, of dear money as a countermeasure against inflationary Government finance is limited. The excess spending of the Government generates both incomes and a supply of money to provide corresponding cash balances. The supply of money replaces the money extinguished by the repayment of traders' indebtedness, and, when the process of repayment reaches its limit, and bank advances are at an irreducible minimum, dear money can do no more.

That is the situation which was met during the war by controls. As we have seen (above, p. 42) the end of the war saw bank advances at a minimum, and stocks of goods (at any rate, of unrationed goods) below the minimum, in that spending was being severely restricted by shop shortages. Inflation had gone far beyond the replacement of the bank advances extinguished, and had created a vast mass of redundant money. The excess money was in the hands of people who, during the war, had been prevented from spending: that is, from replenishing stocks, or from maintaining and renewing plant and property. The holders of it had no need to borrow, and consequently a restriction of credit had not the power to stop excess spending.

The relapse into inflation in the last two years has the same result on a smaller scale. When the excess spending power created by the Government is fed from stocks, the sellers are provided with money to pay for the replenishment of their stocks. The spending may not be on stock-held products; it may, for example, be on services or on capital outlay. But the recipients of the money so spent are in a position to spend it in turn. Except in so far as the money is at some stage withheld from spending and tied up in balances, the spending takes the form in the end of drawing on stocks.

Chapter Five

CAPITAL OUTLAY
AND EXTERNAL INVESTMENT

EXTERNAL INVESTMENT

BUT, it may be asked, has there after all been any relapse
into inflation? The capital outlay of the Government in
1952 was undoubtedly met by a creation of bank money,
but, none the less, the capital resources provided sufficed
on the whole to cover capital outlay. Bank deposits have no
inflationary effect if they are kept idle, and the inflationary
effect is to be measured by excess spending.

It is true that the table of Capital Resources (above, p. 57)
shows for 1952 an excess of resources over capital outlay of
£111 million, and a favourable balance of payments of
£269 million. There is no need to repeat that this result has
been obtained by a re-imposition of import restrictions.
Moreover, the favourable inference drawn assumes that the
proceeds of the exports, visible and invisible, appearing in
the calculation of the balance of payments, are available in
their entirety to pay for the imports. But that is not so. A
part pays for the country's export of capital. External
investment is an 'invisible import', and enters as a debit into
the balance of payments. Under the heading *Overseas
Investment, Borrowing, etc.*, the Balance of Payments White
Paper (Cmd. 8976) includes Government borrowing and
lending, and repayment of Government loans, and sales and
redemptions of investments outside the Sterling Area.
These are partly contractual obligations, but for the rest
are almost entirely acts of policy in which Governments take

93

the initiative. They can be classed with the inter-Governmental grants, such as Marshall Aid, by which the balance of payments difficulties of Great Britain and other countries have been relieved, as Special Resources. From the British point of view Special Resources are a net amount, outgoings, such as Conditional Aid,[1] being set against the receipts.

Under the heading *Overseas Investment* there remains a residuary item, *Other Capital Transactions* (37), which we identify with British external investment.

The special resources are for the most part composed of ascertainable items, and the residual effects on balances and reserves are a matter of exact accounting. When they are deducted from the current balance of payments, the difference representing external investment, is subject to the same errors and uncertainties as the current balance itself.

External investment is a burden on the balance of payments no less than any other kind of spending. If allowance be made for it, the balance is modified as follows:

TABLE XI

	1946	1947	1948	1949	1950	1951	1952
Balance of Payments	− 298	− 443	+ 1	+ 31	+298	− 410	+269
External Investment	− 52	353	342	230	143	296	120
Combined Balance	− 246	− 796	− 341	− 199	+155	− 706	+149

Over the seven years external investments totalled £1,432 million, of which no less than £1,086 million went to the Sterling Area.

[1] Where the equivalent of supplies received by way of Marshall Aid had to be passed on to other participating countries.

The following table shows the special resources:

TABLE XII

	1946	1947	1948	1949	1950	1951	1952
American Loan	149	707	74	—	—	—	—
Canadian Credit	130	105	13	33	16	—	—
Marshall Aid (E.R.P.):							
Grants	—	—	144	244	239	54	—
Loans	—	—	20	57	4	5	—
Conditional Aid, etc.	—	—	- 6	- 46	- 96	—	—
Argentine Railways Sale	—	—	150	—	—	—	—
S. African Gold Loan	—	—	80	- 80	—	—	—
Gifts (Australia and New Zealand)	—	30	—	16	—	—	—
Relief to Germany	- 40	- 81	- 16	- 9	- 3	—	—
Other transactions	86	- 3	1	24	42	- 24	8
	325	758	460	239	202	35	8

The difference between the combined balance and the special resources was reflected in balances and reserves: partly in the reserve of gold and dollars; partly in the externally held sterling; partly in settlements with the Euro-

TABLE XIII

	1946	1947	1948	1949	1950	1951	1952
Capital outlay at home	900	1,160	1,393	1,534	1,674	1,863	2,054
External investment	- 52	353	342	230	143	296	120
Total	848	1,513	1,735	1,764	1,817	2,159	2,174
Capital resources	584	1,074	1,648	1,702	1,743	1,931	2,165
Excess outlay	264	439	87	62	74	228	9
Change in stocks	- 12	+378	+213	+ 65	-183	+506	-165
Residual error	- 6	- 21	+ 41	+ 72	- 46	- 28	+ 7
Combined balance	- 246	-796	-341	-199	+155	-706	+149

pean Payments Union; partly in transactions with the International Monetary Fund.

The inclusion of external investment in the total of spending calls for a restatement of the use of capital resources, as in Table XIII.

THE DOLLAR BALANCE

These calculations are concerned with the over-all balance of payments, and take no account of a separate dollar problem. The next table analyses the combined balance into the balance with the Dollar Area and that with the rest of the world:

TABLE XIV

	1946	1947	1948	1949	1950	1951	1952
Current balance with Dollar Area	− 301	− 510	− 252	− 296	− 80	− 426	− 161
External investment in Dollar Area	− 6	24	44	− 12	− 100	22	− 33
Combined balance with Dollar Area	− 295	− 534	− 296	− 284	+ 20	− 448	− 128
With rest of the world	+ 49	− 262	− 45	+ 85	+135	− 258	+277
Total combined balance	− 246	− 796	− 341	− 199	+155	− 706	+149

Over the seven years the Dollar Area accounts for practically the whole adverse balance of £1,984 million, the net adverse balance with the rest of the world being only £19 million. Moreover, the current dollar balance was only a part of the dollar problem, for there were various transactions with the rest of the world which were settled in gold or dollars. The British Exchange Equalisation Account assumed the responsibility for the foreign exchange transactions of the overseas Sterling Area (subject to certain special arrangements with South Africa). Great Britain also purchased newly mined gold for sterling. And, under Payments Agreements and other arrangements, settlements with countries outside the Dollar Area and the Sterling Area might involve the payment or receipt of gold or dollars; for example a Payments Agreement might require payment in gold if the balance of indebtedness from either party exceeded a specified limit. The following table shows the aggregate dollar debit or credit (in £ millions) year by year:

TABLE XV

	1946	1947	1948	1949	1950	1951	1952
Combined balance with Dollar Area	− 295	− 534	− 296	− 284	+ 20	− 448	− 128
Overseas Sterling Area	− 73	− 306	− 65	− 54	+169	+103	+ 37
Purchase of Gold	+ 82	+ 84	+ 55	+ 68	+100	+ 78	+ 72
Transfer to or from other countries	+ 53	− 198	− 72	− 77	− 5	− 59	− 145
	− 233	− 954	− 378	− 347	+284	− 326	− 164

The Special Resources were nearly all in dollars or gold, and barely sufficed to cover these adverse balances, aggregating £2,118 million.

The line between the over-all balance of payments and the balance of payments with the Dollar Area is not so rigid as is sometimes supposed. The extent to which adverse balances with countries outside the Sterling Area can be settled in sterling is limited and in the five years 1948–52, the net transfers of gold and dollars to these countries have amounted to £358 million. This sum includes payments to them on behalf of the overseas Sterling Area.

An essential factor in this, as well as in the direct balance of payments of the Sterling Area with the Dollar Area, is the competition of British exports with American exports. Not only is the balance of the overseas Sterling Area improved when supplies of manufactures are obtained from

H

Great Britain instead of from the United States, but outside countries, when they make the same substitution, become better supplied with dollars and better placed to play a part in a world of multi-lateral settlements.

If a more severe monetary policy quells over-spending by Great Britain, and relieves the strain on British productive capacity, increased exporting power will be released. Devaluation was intended to have that effect, and when it enabled British exporters to under-sell their American competitors, it might well be that the saving of dollars to the importing countries exceeded the equivalent of the British exports at the new rate of exchange. But the favourable effect was limited owing to the over-employment of British industry, for British manufacturers could not further expand output, and the increase in exports had to be diverted from markets where demand was already insistent. Were the pressure of excess spending relieved, the requisite diversion would become possible. Diminished spending at home would release productive resources for the export market.

Spending at home, however, is not the whole of the trouble. External investment likewise contributed to the total of excess spending. External investment transplants purchasing power from the investing country to the recipient country. Extra demand is engendered in the latter. In the countries of the overseas Sterling Area, which are the principal recipients of British external investment, the extra demand gives rise to a demand for imports, and a part of the imports attracted is sure to be from the Dollar Area. If the external investment ceased, these dollar imports would cease with it. Probably a part of the imports from Great Britain would also cease, but in the existing state of over-employment that would be no disadvantage. Supplies would be released to satisfy the excess spending in other directions.

INVESTMENT IN THE STERLING AREA

Mr. Harrod has laid great stress on the detrimental effect of the export of capital, especially to the Sterling Area, on the British balance of payments,[1] and he has linked the question closely with that of the externally held sterling balances.

The British exchange control, in that it has treated the Sterling Area as a unit, has put no restrictions on the export of capital to any country within it. And the overseas Sterling Area had been kept short of capital during the war in the same way as Great Britain. It was only natural that when British capital resources were reinforced by the American and Canadian loans in 1947, a share should go to meet its requirements. Some went to re-equip British capital enterprises established overseas, the quite considerable surviving part of British external investments, the profits from which still make an important contribution to the economic strength of the country. In the three years 1947–9 British investment in the Sterling Area reached the high total of £741 million. In the following three years, 1950–2, when, no doubt, the demand for capital was becoming less acute, it was £398 million. Even so, it is a substantial item. In the first half of 1953 it was £80 million.

External investment is not all applied to capital outlay: a part is incidental to the expansion of trade. In the annual return of the Balance of Payments 'an attempt is made to record transactions in goods when a change of ownership takes place. . . . It is known that for certain commodities imported into the United Kingdom change of ownership occurs in the country of origin (either before or at shipment). For United Kingdom exports, on the other hand, the transactions are assumed to take place on or after arrival in foreign parts.'[2] It is in virtue of the highly developed mercantile community in Great Britain that to a great extent both exports and imports are British-owned while in

---

[1] See *International Affairs*, April 1950, pp. 153–63, and *The Pound Sterling* (Princeton, 1952), pp. 20–2.
[2] Cmd. 8976, p. 61.

transit. It would seem that, in the official statistical returns, these goods are included in the stocks of the British merchants, and their value is not to be reckoned as an external investment. On the other hand, when time is allowed for payment, any outstanding indebtedness from importers to exporters is an external investment credited to the exporting country. The indebtedness may take the form of simple book debts. But, where it is embodied in bills of exchange, the creditors are the holders for the time being of the bills, and if a bill is acquired by a bank in the debtor's country, the debt to the exporting country is discharged, and the external investment is extinguished. The bank's investment is not external.

Probably the credit outstanding from abroad to British importers in the aggregate is not considerable. Any bills drawn are sterling bills which are discounted and held in London. But the case of British exporters is different. The old established practice by which London banks and accepting houses open sterling acceptance credits in favour of overseas importers still continues, especially in the Sterling Area, though exchange control must have interfered with it elsewhere. Where an importer has been accorded this facility, the exporter draws a bill on the acceptor in pounds sterling, and if the bill is discounted, it is held in London. The importer's debt to the acceptor remains till the bill matures, and constitutes a British investment in the importer's country. Book debts from overseas importers to British exporters (especially to exporters of engineering and constructional products) are also a considerable item.

The growth of British exports from £917 million in 1946 to £2,825 million in 1952 must have been accompanied by a corresponding growth in outstanding commercial credit, against which the growth of imports by approximately the same amount would provide only a small set-off. Commercial credit may have accounted for several hundreds of millions in the total of external investment since the war.

Mr. Harrod, speaking in January 1950,[1] expressed the opinion that a part of the investment in the Sterling Area in 1947, 1948, and the first half of 1949, must be 'capital which goes into the Sterling Area in order, by some way or other, to get beyond the Sterling Area', in other words, to evade the prohibition on the export of capital outside the Sterling Area. That evasion of the exchange control occurred was shown by the activity of the irregular markets in sterling in New York and other foreign countries, but it was not (except temporarily) for the purpose of holding balances of dollars; it was rather for the use of the dollars in obtaining supplies from the Dollar Area, and reaping the advantage of prompt delivery. The speculation against sterling (which had already been reversed at the time when Mr. Harrod was speaking) was mainly effected by quite legitimate methods, delaying purchases from Great Britain and the Sterling Area, and hastening sales, delaying payments in sterling and hastening recovery of payments becoming due.

But anyhow Mr. Harrod's criticism was not confined to the evasion of controls; he contended that 'we should be more modest in our capital aid to the Sterling Area in the short period'.

Writing two years later,[2] he referred again to 'the flow of capital from the United Kingdom to the outer Sterling Area', and commented: 'Some part of it may have been venture capital financing new investment. The greater part probably constituted the withdrawal of capital from Britain by those seeking to diversify their holdings or to avoid the insecurities deemed to beset the holding of capital in the United Kingdom.' He is no longer referring to the illicit use of the Sterling Area as a channel for the transmission of capital to countries outside it, and I feel doubt as to the 'insecurities' of capital in the United Kingdom being a material contributory motive. The venture capital is mainly

---

[1] *International Affairs*, April 1950, p. 161.
[2] *The Pound Sterling*, Princeton, February 1952, p. 21.

in the form of direct investments, and often of extensions and improvements of existing enterprises, and the motive is usually the high profits to be hoped for by those who already possess special knowledge and experience in the development of the places where the enterprises are situated.

Whether it is desirable that this export of capital should cease or diminish is open to question. If its cessation would mean that it would be provided by American enterprise in place of British, the original remittance of the capital sums would of course be an immediate support to the dollar balance of the Sterling Area, but thereafter the profits would become a burden on the balance of payments which import restrictions could not ease.

But investment in the Sterling Area, however desirable it may be, cannot be justified if there is no surplus from which it can be provided.

CREDIT POLICY AND CAPITAL OUTLAY

The effect of tight credit on external investment is very similar to the effect on capital outlay at home. We have seen that the principal impact of dear money is on short-term borrowing for holding stocks of goods. Short-term borrowing is also resorted to in several ways in connection with long-term investment. An industrialist may pay for renewal or extension of his plant by bank advances in anticipation either of future re-invested profits, or of sales of securities from his depreciation fund or reserves, or of a flotation in the investment market. Or, though funds be raised from the investment market, yet the securities may be acquired with borrowed money, either by dealers in the market or by speculators or investors. The speculator borrows for very short periods within which the charge for interest is negligible in comparison with the movements in the prices of the securities he deals in, and he is likely to be impervious to the effects of dear money. The investor who borrows in anticipation of his savings in order to take an opportunity of a favourable investment will expect to be indebted for a longer period, but, even if he expects the total interest he will have to pay for the duration of his loan to exceed the dividends he will receive, the excess is not likely to be a considerable set-off against the capitalised advantages of the investment. And the same is true of a business anticipating its reinvested profits. The deterrent effect of a high short-term rate of interest on capital transactions is small. Also short-term borrowing for the holding of long-term assets (especially of those which are not marketable) is recognised to be imprudent, and those who resort to it are usually anxious anyhow to limit their commitments, both in amount and in time, so that a high interest charge does not greatly reinforce this desire. Except where there is an outbreak of speculation in marketable securities, such as raged in the United States in the years 1926–9, excess spending on capital projects financed by bank advances is not likely to be on a great scale.

Excess spending requires a supply of money in excess of current receipts, but bank advances are not needed by those who already hold surplus balances of money. Indeed, the natural destination of a surplus balance is the investment market; the holder will want to earn interest on any money in excess of a convenient working balance. Keynes laid stress on the possibility that the interest offered by the market on long-term securities might be so low that it would cease to attract investors. That is a contingency quite remote from the post-war conditions and from those of the present day and the foreseeable future. The low rate of interest prevailing up to 1947 was the result of controls preventing the use of money in capital enterprises, and bore no relation to the high yield that could be derived from them (especially from the urgently needed expenditure on arrears of renewals and upkeep of existing enterprises). High yields were characteristic of projects for capital outlay not only at home but abroad. Projects in the Sterling Area were not barred by the exchange control[1] and they competed with projects at home as outlets for the redundant money which had accumulated during the war.

When the demands on the investment market for funds for capital projects exceed the inflow of funds seeking investment, the market lowers the prices of securities (or, in other words, raises the long-term rate of interest), till the resulting deterrent effect on capital enterprise equates capital outlay with the inflow of investible funds. But, if the inflow of funds includes redundant money as well as current savings, the action of the market does not prevent excess spending.

It is evident that, in so far as capital outlay contributes to excess spending, special importance attaches to the existence of redundant money. We saw above (p. 67) that in 1952 progress had been made towards the elimination of redundant money, but was even then incomplete. And inflationary Government finance has since caused a setback. The supply of money is still increasing, for a continued decrease in bank advances during the present year has been insufficient to compensate the increase in Treasury bills and investments.

The deficit in public finance does not necessarily have this inflationary effect: the addition to the supply of money occurs when the banks provide the Government with funds by taking up Treasury bills and other securities. The market for Government securities is in a normally receptive condition, and an understanding might be reached with the banks that, so far as the state of the market permits, they should unload a part of their holdings on investors, and should refrain from subscribing for new issues. The condition as to the state of the market requires some elucidation. The inflow into it of current savings is limited. The purpose of the operation would be to attract surplus money. The surplus money results from the excess spending of the

---

[1] So far as public flotations in the investment market were concerned, the Capital Issues Committee exercised control.

Government: what the Government spends is not covered by what it takes from the taxpayers, and the difference accrues to the taxpayers' cash holdings. Where a taxpayer's cash is raised above a convenient working balance, the excess is likely to seek an opening in the investment market. The redundant money that exists is the result of accumulations in the past; it has failed to be employed in capital enterprise, partly because controls have restricted capital outlay, partly also because the over-employment of industry has held up projects for want of any free productive resources to carry them out. No doubt the external investment which has occurred from 1947 onward is to be accounted for partly by the overflow of investible funds which could not be employed at home.

If the surplus money were drawn off into long-term Government securities, so that the bank deposits embodying it were extinguished, the volume of funds seeking investment would be limited to current savings, and the requirements of external investment would have to compete with those of investment at home for the available resources.

GOVERNMENT SECURITIES AND THE INVESTMENT MARKET

A substantial part of the demand for Government securities emanates from industrial and commercial concerns accumulating reserves of reinvested profits. These reserves are destined ultimately to be spent on desirable improvements and extensions of plant or equipment, and are therefore placed in medium-term securities, which will provide a capital sum on maturity, or can be sold without serious capital loss if needed sooner.

Are not such securities the equivalent of loose cash? Is anything to be gained by the substitution of them for bank deposits? There is a material difference. If they are sold before maturity, buyers must be found. If there is a heavy pressure of sales on the market, there will be a substantial fall of prices even of medium-term securities. If we are supposing all redundant money to have been absorbed into securities by an initial operation, buyers with surplus cash cannot be immediately found to take up an exceptional volume of sales. Some will have to procure bank advances. If policy is aiming at eliminating redundant money, additional bank advances will not be readily allowed. Moreover, neither speculators nor speculative investors concern themselves with Government securities. If anyone buys gilt-edged securities with borrowed money it is the stockjobber,[1] whose functions in making a market compel him to be a speculator in whatever securities he holds. And the stockjobber aims at so regulating the prices he quotes that he will never find himself buying more than he wants of any security.

So long as the banks abstain from buying securities on their own account, the market in Government securities will be limited; sellers must find buyers who are able and willing to pay for them from their own resources. If there is no redundant money, the sellers must compete with sellers of shares and with new flotations for so much as they can attract of current savings.

When almost the whole of the National Debt was funded like Consols, that is, repayable only at the option of the Government, this state of the market was easily induced. But at the present time maturities are a complication: maturing securities ensure to the market from time to time huge supplies of cash which the Government has to raise either from the investment market or from the banks. If many of the holders of the maturing securities prefer to have cash, it may be difficult to find new holders. Either a portion of the new securities must be taken by the banks, or money must be raised by Treasury bills to pay off the old. New money is created in the hands of the holders who have been paid off, and who may be presumed to want it for capital outlay or other form of spending. Excess spending revives.

[1] Underwriters of new issues, who have to take more than they anticipated, may have to borrow. There are also speculators in new gilt-edged issues, 'stags', who hope to resell at a small profit.

The problem of maturities is not so baffling as appears at first sight, because a portion of the maturing securities would be already held by the banks, and their replacement by new securities would not add to the stock of money. And among the companies holding maturing securities in their reserves will be many which do not contemplate early capital outlays, and will take up new securities in their place. But at a time when the Government relies on borrowing to meet its own capital outlay, its obligation to repay maturing loans is an additional difficulty in the way of avoiding inflation.

It is a mistake to consider excess spending on capital at home and abroad separately from excess spending on the active accumulation of stocks. If tight credit turns active accumulation into a negative quantity, so that traders cut down their orders to producers with a view to reducing their stocks, not only is the congestion of orders relieved and the importation of goods to maintain stocks diminished, but bank advances decrease along with stocks, and the supply of money contracts. The contraction might be sufficient of itself to eliminate the redundant money, but, if it is not, it is for budgetary policy to redeem an appropriate amount of the securities in the hands of the banks. The necessary money, if surplus revenue is not made available, must be raised by flotations of Government securities in the investment market. It was for this purpose that I advocated a forced loan at the end of the war, when the redundant money amounted to thousands of millions of pounds. Now that it is a more manageable amount, loans voluntarily subscribed should meet the case.

So long as an excess demand prevails, producers endeavour to extend output not only by employing more labour but also by installing more plant. They want to extend capacity and, in face of the scarcity of labour, to provide more labour-saving mechanism. Government flotations have to compete with these openings for capital outlay. When tighter credit discourages active accumulation, and lightens the pressure of demand, these rival openings become less attractive, and the market for Government securities is improved.

A policy of eliminating redundant money obviously includes the avoidance of an inflationary finance which would generate redundant money anew. Otherwise, as we have seen, the efficacy of tight credit is limited.

Given prudent public finance, it would be for credit policy to regulate the supply of money by influencing the acceptable level of stocks. If an adverse balance of payments threatened, dear money would discourage active accumulation. If unemployment[1] threatened, cheap money would encourage active accumulation. If unemployment and an adverse balance appear together, a reduction of costs in terms of foreign money units is needed: either a reduction of wages or a devaluation.

OVERSEAS STERLING BALANCES

Elimination of redundant money, combined with an adequate credit policy, would put an end to the adverse balance of payments, but only to the over-all adverse balance. What of the adverse dollar balance? We have seen that the two are not wholly independent of one another, but we cannot go so far as to conclude that a cessation of overspending, and of the adverse over-all balance of payments to which it gives rise, would automatically solve the dollar problem.

If it did not, the remedy would be a stronger dose. A favourable over-all balance would result, in which the transactions with the Dollar Area would get their share. We are reckoning external investment as a debit or invisible import in the balance of payments, so a favourable balance means a receipt of cash, if not in dollars, then in sterling, or in credit with the European Payments Union.

[1] That is, unemployment due to an insufficient flow of money, not unemployment due to non-monetary causes.

A gradual reduction of the externally held sterling would certainly be a step towards normal conditions. This sterling, in so far as it exceeds what the holders' convenience would require, is a form of 'redundant money'; it provides them with the means of over-spending. Exchange control prevents the spending of it outside the Sterling Area, and the over-spending is, therefore, concentrated on imports from the Sterling Area, and especially from Great Britain. Overseas sterling balances have been an important contributory cause of the congestion of orders and of the over-employment of British industry. The total of externally held sterling (other than that held by the International Monetary Fund and the International Bank) has fluctuated since 1945 but is now (30th June 1953) on balance very little changed. But the amount held in the Colonies has risen from £454 million on 31st December 1945 to £1,133 million. The amount held in the rest of the Sterling Area has been reduced from £2,008 million to £1,758 million, and in the rest of the world from £1,232 million to £716 million.

The increase in the Colonies is no doubt in great part attributable to the dependence of the Colonies on London for the management of their currencies. How much of their sterling is tied up in currency reserves is not disclosed. But the Colonies have, of course, conformed to the general monetary expansion which has occurred in the Sterling Area since 1939. And the expansion has presumably been proportionally greater in countries in course of rapid development.

The expansive tendency has been accelerated since the devaluation of 1949. The Colonies are largely producers of primary products, the prices of which responded more easily and quickly to devaluation than those of manufactures. And hard on devaluation came the Korean War, and the spectacular rise in the dollar prices of materials associated with rearmament and strategic stock-piling. The rise in the sterling holdings of the Colonies from £574 million in June 1949 to £1,035 million in June 1952 reflects a rise in their monetary circulation, though mention should be made of the continued rise to £1,133 million in June 1953, in spite of the fall in prices of materials. The sterling balances held by countries other than the Colonies still stand at a formidable total, £2,474 million, being not far short of the equivalent of a year's British exports.

Among the beneficial consequences of devaluation, or at any rate, among those which have afforded some relief to this country, is to be reckoned the depreciation of the wealth-value of the overseas sterling balances. The method by which relief has been obtained is not very different from that of the unjust steward. To the debtor who owed a hundred measures of oil, he said, 'take thy bond and sit down quickly and write fifty'.

Sterling, it is true, was not the same thing as oil. Its value was admittedly a matter of British legal enactment, and holders must be deemed to have been aware of the possibility of its being altered by unilateral action. Forgery such as the unjust steward recommended was not involved.

Actually a part of the sterling held outside the Sterling Area was subject to a gold guarantee, so that £75 million had to be provided by way of revaluation payments in the years 1949–51 (in addition to £173 million which had to be paid to the International Monetary Fund and Bank).

Chapter Six

PROSPECTS AND POLICIES

INFLATION AND THE WAGE LEVEL

IN my book *Economic Rebirth* (March 1946) I pointed out that up to that time some of the countries holding large amounts of sterling had undergone a much greater degree of inflation than Great Britain, and I suggested that their currencies should be devalued in terms of sterling. The increase in the value of their sterling in terms of their own money units would have been a windfall, a book debt to a central bank or a currency board, the funding of which could readily have been arranged.[1]

If, on the other hand, the rates of exchange within the Sterling Area were held sacrosanct, the alternative to a painful reversal of inflation in those parts of the Sterling Area where inflation had got out of hand would be a resort to inflation in Great Britain. That, I estimated, might mean reducing the wealth-value of the pound sterling by half. If the wage level be taken as a criterion, the pound had already lost one-third of its value since 1939. And I anticipated further that a reduction by half (to one-third of the pre-war purchasing power), even if it could be stopped at that level, would cause a catastrophic dislocation of economic relations.

This hypothetical contingency has approximately been realised. At the time of devaluation in 1949 the index of weekly wages (100 in 1938) had risen to 180. It has since risen to 228. But an index of weekly wage rates understates the rise. Hours have been reduced, but hours actually

[1] *Economic Rebirth*, pp. 84–7.

worked remain much the same, and there is so much the more overtime pay. Average weekly earnings in manufacturing industry have risen from 50s. 4d. in 1938 to 150s. 10d. in 1952. And the tale is still unfinished. Indeed, as was shown above (p. 65), the increase in wages in Great Britain has been very little more than in the United States. Nearly all the adjustment required by the rise of 44 per cent. in the sterling value of the American dollar has still to be made.

And we are only too conscious of the dislocation caused. Every bargain or regulation fixing payments in money comes up for revision over and over again: wages, salaries, controlled rents; charges for travelling and transport, for postage and telephones, and for public utilities; limits for pecuniary penalties and means tests. The financial provision for any future purpose is exposed to disappointment. Pensions, pension funds, life insurance and annuities, fail to afford the standard of living planned for their beneficiaries. The benefits secured under National Insurance schemes against sickness, unemployment and old age, are found inadequate. The activities of learned societies and philanthropic institutions have to be curtailed as the purchasing power of nominally fixed endowments shrinks. Industrial concerns find that the value of depreciation funds and reserves which they have accumulated in money or in fixed interest investments, has disastrously declined in terms of renewals and extensions of plant, for which the funds were intended.

Each successive rise in the wage level is viewed by the public with some misgiving. And rightly, because the resistance that may be expected to any reduction of wages makes the rise irrevocable. It marks a new and irreversible step towards a further inflation, and a further instalment of the dislocations and embarrassments which inflation involves.

But, when a rate of exchange has been fixed, which requires a big rise of wages as a condition of a restoration of equilibrium, should not every rise which makes for progress towards that end be welcomed? It should, *provided*, on the one hand, that the rate of exchange is not liable to be altered, and, on the other, that the wealth-value of the foreign unit to which the rate of exchange links the money, is not liable to rise. As to the former condition, if we can look forward to a time when the dollar value of the pound can be raised, the wage level then prevailing will determine how far it can be raised without causing unemployment.

As to the latter condition, a heavy fall in the American price level would mean a corresponding fall in the equilibrium dollar value of the pound. If a rise in the British wage level had so depressed this equilibrium value that it was little above the officially established rate of exchange, the fall in the American price level (in other words, the rise in the wealth-value of the dollar) might require a further devaluation in order to avoid an adverse balance or unemployment or both.

Apprehensions are often expressed as to the repercussions upon Great Britain of a possible decline of activity in the United States. A decline of activity would be a consequence of a shrinkage of demand, a diminished flow of dollars, falling prices and profits, unemployment, reduced demand for materials. The reduced demand for primary products in both quantity and price would adversely affect the balance of payments of the overseas Sterling Area (as in 1949). And American industry would tend to unload surplus output and surplus stocks of finished products on foreign markets, with injurious consequences to competing exporters in Great Britain, and elsewhere. If on the occurrence of such an event the pound were still substantially under-valued, export prices, though unremunerative to those whose costs were reckoned in dollars, might still be profitable to British producers, who would so be able to maintain their sales against American competition.[1]

[1] There might be an interval during which American traders were unloading stocks at a loss so recklessly as to demoralise markets. But the interval would surely be short. Selling goods at prices which are definitely short of the minimum cost of replacement is an act of panic, when credit has broken down, and cash must be procured at any cost to stave off bankruptcy.

I

If the under-valuation of the pound be supposed to have ceased, or to be more than offset by the collapse of American prices, further devaluation, or rather an abandonment of the fixed rate of exchange, would be the right remedy. Depreciation of the money unit, as in 1931, is the right policy when exporters' costs have become excessive.

AN UP-VALUATION OF THE POUND

The under-valuation of the pound is itself a potent cause of over-employment. A policy of extinguishing the redundant money fails of its full effect unless the under-valuation is dealt with. The under-valuation might be ended in one or more of three ways:

(1) a fall in the American price level;
(2) a continued rise of the British wage level;
(3) a revision of the rate of exchange.

Of the first there is no immediate prospect. Any setback to the inflationary tendency in America is likely to be slight in comparison with the existing under-valuation of the pound.

The second would probably be a very slow process. It would continue over a prolonged transitional period, throughout which the country would suffer from the injurious effects of progressive inflation, and from the weakness due to over-employment.

The third, an up-valuation of the pound, would be a direct and immediate remedy. But its practical application would not be free from difficulty.

In the first place, variations in rates of exchange are not easily reconcilable with membership of the International Monetary Fund. One of the primary purposes of the Fund is to promote exchange stability, and it only allows a change of parity of a money unit in case of a 'fundamental disequilibrium'. The Fund readily agreed to devaluation in 1949. It might not so easily accept an up-valuation, which could be represented as imputing weakness to the American dollar, or as admitting the devaluation to have been a mistake.

Moreover, it is hardly possible to arrive at an appropriate rate of exchange by a single step. It can only be attained by a process of trial and error. The need to make a succession of tentative changes before deciding on a permanent parity was recognised when the Fund at its initiation postponed the determination of the parity of the French franc, and allowed France a free hand for the time being.

The logical sequel to the selection of a rate of exchange which at a given moment maintains equilibrium between the pound and the dollar would be a policy of altering the rate at every subsequent moment at which a change in wealth-value of the dollar disturbs the equilibrium—a policy which would be, superficially, at any rate, irreconcilable with the Fund's purpose of promoting 'exchange stability'. If the consent of the Fund to an up-valuation of the pound were not forthcoming, and Great Britain resigned from the Fund, the effect on Anglo-American relations might be unfortunate. The Fund was essentially an American creation, embodying American ideas; nothing of Keynes's proposals was accepted which did not accord with those ideas.

Given the consent of the Fund, an up-valuation would still not be free from complications. A sudden alteration of the dollar value of the pound would upset the calculations of all who held assets actually or potentially valued in dollars against liabilities reckoned in pounds. For some primary products the American demand is so great a proportion of the world demand that the world price is practically a dollar price, and a fall in the sterling equivalent of the dollar would leave the dollar price little changed; producers and holders in the Sterling Area would sustain a loss. If the up-valuation were confined to Great Britain, and the rest of the Sterling Area retained rates of exchange on the United States unaltered, the loss would fall only on traders in Great

Britain holding primary products destined for sale in over-seas markets. The trader might have hedged by effecting a forward sale in sterling of goods equivalent to his holding. But hedging would not avoid the loss; it would only shift it on to the forward buyers. The forward buyers who provide hedging facilities in the great commodity markets have broad shoulders. They are professional speculators who are accustomed to take the rough with the smooth, but a heavy unforeseen loss falling on the market as a whole might have serious consequences. They could themselves hedge against a change in the rate of exchange by means of forward purchases of sterling against dollars. I do not suppose they would ordinarily do so, but if an up-valuation of the pound became a recognised possibility, they would probably take this precaution. There would then be a speculative demand for sterling.

In the event of an up-valuation, British exporters of manufactured goods would find the dollar equivalent of their costs suddenly raised. Some (probably a large majority) would find that they could sell all they could produce at the higher dollar price. But undoubtedly there would be some who, having been tempted into the export market by the high sterling prices secured them by devaluation, could not raise their dollar price, and would be compelled wholly or partly to abandon their export markets.

It would, of course, be undesirable to push the appreciation of sterling either beyond the point at which the productive resources thus displaced from export markets could find an outlet in the home market, or beyond the point at which the gain in the dollar proceeds of the surviving exports would outweigh the proceeds of the exports which would cease.

If, therefore, a rise in the dollar value of the pound were decided on, it would be wise to proceed gradually. In applying the process of trial and error, it would not be necessary at the first trial to fix a rate of exchange estimated, as nearly as might be, to be ultimately just right, which when put to the test of experience would be as likely to be found too high as too low. It would be better to raise the rate by successive small amounts, so that the immediate disturbance would not be too great, and to stop when unfavourable reactions began to be felt.

It would be well, first of all, to prepare the ground by bringing the requisite monetary and fiscal measures into full effect. Redundant money should be eliminated by taxation, combined with loans calculated to attract the long-term investor, and credit should be so regulated as to prevent a recrudescence of redundant money or of excess spending.

It was pointed out above (p. 108) that the maintenance of an over-all favourable balance by these measures would not by itself be enough to ensure a favourable balance with the Dollar Area, and that if they are pushed far enough to eliminate any dollar debit, they might give rise to a substantial favourable balance with the rest of the world. In these conditions there would be an upward pressure on the foreign exchange value of the pound, which would be all the greater if there were a resumption of monetary expansion in the United States. There would be a growing accumulation of reserves.

An appreciation of the pound would ensue, which, if permitted, would carry the rate of exchange above the upper limit of $2·82 at present in operation. If it is true that the pound is under-valued at that rate, appreciation would be found to make the balance of payments all the more favourable, and suspension of the limit would open the way to a gradual rise of the pound up to the rate corresponding to comparative costs.

That process presupposes a 'floating pound' such as prevailed from 1931 to 1939. A floating pound does not mean a rate of exchange free from any Government interference, and following market impulses from day to day and from hour to hour. The Exchange Equalisation Account was established in order to prevent undesirable short-term fluctuations in the rate, an essential precaution to guard against a casual movement starting a vicious circle of monetary expansion or contraction. But the rate of exchange (that is to say, the dollar rate, which determines gold parity) should be so determined by the Bank of England (being the agent of the Government) as to maintain steady progress towards the equilibrium rate. If every rise in the rate were allowed only in response to a palpable market tendency, opposition from the United States and the International Monetary Fund would probably be diminished, if not altogether disarmed.

WAGES AND EXPORT COSTS

The alternative to variation in the gold parity or dollar value of the pound is a continuance of the rise in wages and prices, up to the point at which the under-valuation of the pound is ended by the rise in costs. That would almost certainly be a prolonged process, during which the country would continue to suffer both from the over-employment which causes the existing weakness of the balance of payments, and from the vexations and dislocations of chronic inflation.

And whereas the rate of exchange can be adjusted by official action, the movements of the wage level are not easily controlled. When the authorities judge the rate of exchange to have reached its resting point, they can refrain from further increases, and leave the economic affairs of the country to adjust themselves to the rate. But when the wage level is believed to have attained parity of costs, there is no reliable or ready way to stop further increases. There are sure to be anomalies calling for further wage increases here and there to restore relativities, and it is only too likely that some of these increases will go beyond what is justifiable and will give rise to a new set of anomalies. A rise of the wage level and therefore of costs beyond such as would correspond with foreign costs at the existing rates of exchange would constitute a 'fundamental disequilibrium' warranting a new devaluation. Inflation might thus be extended indefinitely.

It may perhaps be argued that a general rise of wages has an advantage over an up-valuation of the pound in that while the latter affects all export industries indiscriminately, the former would be selective; the rise of wages in any industry would be limited to what the industry could stand. But surely that advantage would not last long. Under conditions of full employment industries compete with one another for labour, and wages in any industry cannot lag far or for long behind a general rise.

Is it possible that after all British exporters will be found unable to stand any increase in costs? In that case any further general rise of wages would cause unemployment. Not only is the present abnormally low level of unemployment a symptom of over-employment, but there is plenty of evidence that delay in deliveries is still a real obstacle to British export trade.

Exporters, however, have to face the prospect of increased competition from Germany and Japan. Germany is not over-employed. Nevertheless the million unemployed cannot all be counted as a labour reserve available to enlarge the capacity of the export industries. The extent to which the West German economic system has succeeded in absorbing the millions of refugees and immigrants is a notable achievement, but the process is not easily accelerated. The fears so often expressed of German competition are usually based on the supposition that subsidies and artificial aids are being or will be given to the German exporters. But of course the under-valuation of the pound is a very direct incentive to the exporters of competing nations to ask for such assistance. And in the United States the low costs of British producers in terms of dollars are a powerful support to the claims of the American industries in competition with them for high protective tariffs. The great mass-producing American industries have little to fear from foreign competitors, but the small concerns which produce individuality products cannot easily hold their own against rivals paying for highly qualified labour wages at a third or a quarter of American rates. In a country whose industry specialises in mass-production, economic life tends to become one-sided, and the diversification which a protective tariff on individuality products brings about is an undeniable social benefit, even at the cost of some departure from the ideal international division of labour.

British exporters must undoubtedly be prepared to face competition in international markets. And the problem of future rates of exchange will not be unaffected by the competitive conditions. But till a stop has been put to the excess spending which causes an adverse balance of payments, it is useless to look for a solution of the problem.

THE NEAR FUTURE

The favourable balance recorded in the first half of 1953 offers little ground for reassurance. It was maintained by means of import restrictions, one important part of which, those on imports from Western Europe, is in course of being relaxed. Against the increase of £186 million in the gold and dollar reserves in the half-year must be set the increase of £172 million in sterling liabilities.

The favourable balance is narrow and precarious. What then are the future prospects? And, more particularly, what is being done in the region of monetary and fiscal policy to cope with excess spending?

Bank rate was reduced on the 17th September from 4 per cent. to $3\frac{1}{2}$ per cent. The reduction was greeted with lively satisfaction in financial circles, and prices of Government securities were marked up to an extent which marked the reduction as foreshadowing a period of cheap money, rather than as a token of future flexibility of the rate. The mere fact that the token of flexibility took the form of a reduction of the rate rather than of an increase, could be interpreted as a sign of official optimism. The optimism is assumed by the public to be founded on an expert estimation of the various trends.

But is that assumption correct?

We have seen that the budget for 1953–4 provides a surplus of only £109 million against anticipated capital disbursements by the Government of £549 million, and also that the financial measures of October 1953 contained no clear promise of raising money for the deficiency from other sources than the banks. Redundant money is being once more generated. Bank deposits in November 1953 were £6,183 million, compared with £5,963 million twelve months earlier, although advances and commercial bills had been reduced by £70 million in that period; financial accommodation to the amount of £320 million had been found for the Government.

The budget of 1953–4 was one of tax reductions. The budget of 1952–3 had made immediate tax reductions amounting to £107 million net, and estimated to cost a further £45 million in a full year, but it imposed the Excess Profits Levy, the yield of which, while negligible in the first year, was expected to amount in a full year to £100 million net (after allowing for the associated adjustments in the yield of Profits Tax and Income Tax). It was no doubt this measure that accounted for the addition of £120 million to tax reserves in 1952.

The immediate tax reliefs granted in 1953–4 were reckoned to be £169 million. But in subsequent years the repeal of the Excess Profits Levy (from 1st January 1954) was estimated to cause a loss of revenue ultimately of £125 million in a full year, and the restoration of initial depreciation allowances (at lower rates than before the suspension in 1952) was to cost the revenue £50 million 1954–5 and thereafter £84 million in a full year. So much of the reduction of 6d. in the income tax as related to profits would only begin to take effect in 1954.

There will therefore probably be found to have been a very large reduction in tax reserves in the course of 1953.

Corresponding to the anticipations of additional taxation which strengthened the country's capital resources in 1951, there will have been anticipations of tax reliefs which will have weakened them in 1953. A reduction of capital resources, unless accompanied by a reduction of the rate of capital formation, would aggravate the evil of excess spending. It will increase the difficulty of obtaining money for the Government's loans from genuine savings.

Excess spending, it may be said, is merely another name for inflation. If the existing rate of exchange is to be taken as set policy, and if the under-valuation of the pound is bound to lead to inflation, where is the harm in following a budgetary policy which leads in the same direction?

It is true that excess spending is an essential stage in the process of inflation. But there is a fundamental difference between the two cases, where inflation is generated from within a country and where from outside. Where it is from within, the inflationary tendency starts from excess spending, whether by the Government or by traders or individuals, and a rise of prices, an adverse balance of payments and a depreciation of the money follow.

But where inflation starts abroad, and is communicated through the foreign exchanges the phases are different. The first impact is felt in increased sales abroad, and a *favourable* balance of payments. The country then has the choice between letting the favourable balance generate an additional monetary reserve, and indulging in a monetary expansion, which will give rise to excess spending, and put an end to the favourable balance.

The under-valuation of the pound puts Great Britain in some respects in the position of a country receiving the contagion of inflation from abroad. But the position is complicated by the presence of redundant money and by the excessive degree of the under-valuation.

The redundant money, even when it was not being added to by a renewal of inflationary finance, provided the means of an excess spending which attracted imports and caused an adverse balance. The effect of the excessive devaluation was so to lower the prices of exports that the favourable effect normally to be expected from a depreciation of the money unit on the balance of payments was nullified by the fall in the total dollar value of their proceeds. Great Britain is thus suffering from the weakness arising from an internal inflation, and yet is deprived of the remedy which a depreciation of the pound would normally afford, if the rate of exchange had previously been in equilibrium. This weakness is the source of the recurrent crises, which have to be dealt with by restrictions of imports. As soon as the balance of payments ceases to be adverse, the Government of the day supposes that the crisis has been surmounted, and relaxes the restrictions.

So long as the underlying weakness, the excess spending, persists, the relaxation is sure to lead to another crisis. At the present time, the Government is not only about to restore the liberalisation of trade with Western Europe, but is also putting an end to rationing. Rationing is itself a form of import restriction; it played an important part, along with the export drive and the restriction of imports of unrationed products, in Sir Stafford Cripps's policy of austerity.

In place of Cripps's policy, the present Government have suppressed a great part of the food subsidies. But they have made more than equivalent remissions of taxation, and have left the budget position gravely weakened. So far as the tax remissions have reduced the burden on profits and high incomes, the loss of capital resources is likely to be in great part balanced by an increase in private saving. But even the advantage of increased savings will be largely lost unless the Government draws upon the investment market to finance its own capital outlay, instead of having recourse to the banks.

BANK RATE AND GOVERNMENT SECURITIES

But, it may be contended, if the Government wants to raise money from the investment market, will not a low Bank rate be deemed indispensable?

A short-sighted view. Nothing can be more adverse to the market for Government flotations than a state of over-spending. For the demand for investible funds for capital outlay is derived from the current demand for products in general. When that demand outruns productive power, producers seek to extend capacity by installing additional plant, and, when they are confronted by a shortage of labour, they resort to labour-saving mechanisms. A low Bank rate, by encouraging active accumulation, and so expanding demand, intensifies the competition of capital outlay with Government flotations for investible funds. A high Bank rate on the other hand reduces active accumulation, and the resulting decline in demand diminishes the inducement to producers to extend capacity, and slackens their competition for the capital resources of the market.

And when inflation has become so manifest that investors begin to take account of the wealth-value of money, their distrust of the value of a future income fixed in money units is reflected in the price of fixed interest securities. The yield of 5 per cent. War Loan in the autumn of 1920 rose above 6 per cent. The yield of French Government securities in the summer of 1926 exceeded 10 per cent. In the former case it was twelve months of dear money, with Bank rate at 7 per cent., that restored confidence in the pound, so that Government securities settled down to a yield of $4\frac{1}{2}$ per cent. In the latter case it was Poincaré's drastic financial programme that restored confidence in the franc.

The long-term rate of interest at the present time does not seem to be seriously raised by want of confidence in the wealth-value of the pound. The very low rate which obtained during and immediately after the war was attributable to the controls which restricted capital outlay and so limited the demands upon investible funds. The rise from $2\frac{1}{2}$ per cent. in 1946 to $4\frac{1}{2}$ per cent. in 1952 was no doubt due to the relaxation of the controls and the impact of the high demand for capital resources upon the market.

If active accumulation of stocks were extinguished by tight credit, and the congestion of orders to producers were thus ended, the excessive demand from industry for capital resources would cease, and the Government could readily draw away the excess supply of money into long-term or funded loans. Experience has shown that this process actually lowers the long-term rate of interest. A high Bank rate, at its first impact, causes a fall in the prices of securities. But a fall of, say, 2 or 3 per cent. in the price means a very small rise in the yield: if the previous yield of a security at its market price was 4 per cent., the yield becomes 4·08 or 4·12 per cent. The rise is soon far more than offset by the reduction of the pressure to raise capital.

FULL EMPLOYMENT AND OVER-EMPLOYMENT

But, it will be objected, does not the same operation which relieves the pressure on the investment market give rise to unemployment? And the answer must be that, *if pushed too far*, it does. Hence the vital need for a flexible Bank rate.

There is nothing new in that. Flexibility was taken for granted in the nineteenth century. Insufficient flexibility was largely responsible for the disastrous mismanagement of Bank rate in the inter-war period, 1919–39.

A high Bank rate is needed at the present time, but it would probably not have to last long. It should continue till the state of congestion of orders and over-employment has been brought to an end. Undeniably *some* increase in the numbers unemployed would be likely to result.

The fact is that a state of excess demand for labour or over-employment reduces the actual numbers unemployed below what would ordinarily be regarded as a minimum.

Lord Beveridge in his *Full Employment in a Free Society* formed a rough estimate of the percentage of unemployed corresponding to full employment. He took full employment to mean, in some degree at any rate, over-employment: 'it means having always more vacant jobs than unemployed men, not slightly fewer jobs' (p. 18). With that assumption he made some very broad calculations leading to an estimate of 3 per cent. 'as a conservative, rather than an unduly hopeful, aim to set for the average unemployment rate for the future under conditions of full employment' (p. 128). And applying the percentage to a total including 'a substantial body of persons with practically no risk either of seasonal or of interval unemployment', he indicated a figure of 550,000 unemployed. This calculation he made when quite aware that 'in war it has proved possible to cut the unemployed margin down to $\frac{1}{2}$ per cent. or less'.

Lord Beveridge's standard of 3 per cent. may be compared with the actual numbers unemployed in the past four years:

TABLE XVI

	1949	1950	1951	1952
Number unemployed (thousands) ...	308	314	253	414
Civil labour force (millions) ...	22·0	22·3	22·4	22·5
Percentage ...	1·4	1·4	1·1	1·8

The Committee of Experts who reported to the United Nations in December 1949 on *National and International Measures for Full Employment* recommended the adoption of a 'Full Employment Target', which, 'according to the circumstances of each country, may be defined as a range (e.g., from 2 to 4 per cent., or from 3 to 5 per cent. of wage-earners) rather than as a precise figure' (para. 145).

I myself in 1936, after mentioning the fall in the percentage of unemployment from 23 in August 1932 to 12 in August 1936, remarked: 'No one can say with any confidence what percentage is to be regarded as "normal" under existing conditions. I do not think we ought to be satisfied with a ratio above 4 per cent.'[1]

In 1946 when the Government instructed the Government Actuary to make the calculations on which the National Insurance was to be based, they seem to have had no faith in estimates made by those who really believed in the means of maintaining full employment. They instructed the Actuary to assume an average rate of unemployment of 8½ per cent. The result was a large surplus on National Insurance Funds, reaching £169 million per annum in 1950 (when the expenditure on unemployment benefit was £16 million), and the estimate was revised in 1951.

Whatever the standard of 'normal' may be, it is certain that the present percentage of unemployment is substantially below it.

Is not this a highly desirable state of things? Ought it not to be perpetuated?

Several different causes have contributed to over-employment. Among them, immediately after the war, price control and redundant money were the principal, and easy credit reinforced the effects of redundant money. With rising wages and a rising American price level, price control lost much of its efficacy and in 1949 devaluation brought into operation the under-valuation of the pound.

At the present time the first place among these causes should perhaps be accorded to the under-valuation of the pound. Under-valuation means that British costs, that is to say, British wages, are unduly low in terms of foreign money units, such as dollars. The production of foreign trade products, that is to say, exportable and importable goods, offers opportunities of expanded sales and high profits. The advantage of enjoying these opportunities accrues to the employers of labour at the relatively low rates of British wages, and is therefore reflected in that intensified demand for labour which we call over-employment.

[1] *Lessons of Monetary Experience*, edited by A. D. Gayer (New York, 1937), p. 134.

Advocates of over-employment would hardly wish to have it at the cost of a depression of the wage level, and the experience of the last four years has shown that the low wage level initiated by devaluation does not last: the same competition for labour which is manifested in over-employment takes effect in a marked tendency of wages to rise.

And, so long as wages remain depressed, the same desire to extend sales, which gives rise to the intensified competition for labour, leads to exports being sold too cheap. The adverse terms of trade so caused constitute a loss of real wealth to the country.

Therefore, the idea of a policy of perpetuating over-employment by an under-valuation of the pound in terms of foreign money units, is hardly to be entertained; it is neither practicable nor desirable.

But there are other methods of inducing over-employment. They may be grouped together under the general head of over-spending. Over-spending is the underlying cause of inflation; both of active inflation, taking effect in rising prices and wages, and of suppressed inflation, held in check by price control. Whether the inflationary tendency be attributable to imprudent Government finance, or to a relaxation of credit, or to the presence of redundant money, it originates in each case in excess spending.

In existing economic conditions there is no difficulty in continuing the inflationary tendency and the resulting over-employment, provided the country is willing to face the consequences. But the consequences are surely unattractive—not to say, repellent.

To most people called upon to form an opinion the undesirability of active inflation is axiomatic. The fundamental objection to it, it is true, is the dislocation and injustice caused by the degradation of money, the rise of prices and wages; and, in the first instance, the effect of over-spending is the depletion of stocks, before there is any rise of prices. The rise of prices can be further postponed so long as imported supplies can be had to replenish stocks. But eventually the excess of imports will threaten to exhaust the monetary reserves, and a restriction of imports will become unavoidable. The interval of over-spending at unchanged prices is short. And it is but little prolonged at the cost of that weakness in the balance of payments which has been the country's obsessing post-war problem.

The policy of price control, followed during the war, and continued after it in the hope of reconciling a monetary expansion with unchanging prices, failed in face of redundant money, uncontrolled wages and American inflation. And price control, in so far as it succeeds, actually aggravates the trouble of over-spending.

In any case, price control is difficult to enforce and make effective. The excess imports have to be stopped by restrictions. The effect of over-spending is then concentrated on the shortage of stocks. The enforcement of price control inevitably requires a reimposition of rationing, but rationing cannot be applied to everything. Where rationing cannot be applied, spending is restricted by shop shortages. People cannot spend because they cannot get what they want. In the case of an unrationed product in short supply, evasion of the price control is to the interest not only of sellers but even of buyers, who are glad to pay a higher price rather than fail to get the goods.

It is a mistake to regard inflation as an infallible means of maintaining over-employment. Over-employment results from the desire of producers to extend their output to take advantage of an expanding market at existing prices. It depends on the attractiveness of the existing prices, and therefore the producers' confidence in the value of money. A policy which relies on progressive inflation to perpetuate over-employment is bound eventually to come to grief through discredit of the money. An attempt to enforce price control is likely to aggravate the discredit. In Germany in the years between the end of the war and the monetary reform of 1948, the discredit of money was such that it dropped out of use, and barter became the rule. A certain

K

portion of wages was paid in money and was accepted in payment for rationed foods. For any other purpose the purchasing power of this money wage was derisory. Under such conditions industrial activity was reduced to an extremely low level.

Inflation would have to go a long way to reach such a stage in England or America. But there might quite possibly develop such a state of discredit of the money that over-employment would no longer be maintained. Producers would refuse to accept orders without a price variation clause which the traders offering the orders would be unwilling to give.

A MONETARY STANDARD

'Full' employment, a permanent state of the labour market in which there is no unemployment attributable to monetary causes, is attainable. In the past departures from full employment have occurred when a monetary expansion has gone too far, and has had to be not merely stopped but reversed. The reversal, taking the form of a contraction of the flow of money, 'deflation', inflicted a decline of demand and a fall of prices, which made industry unremunerative at the existing level of wages. Unemployment and falling wages ensued.

If an excessive monetary expansion were never allowed to occur, there need never be a deflation. What kind of monetary expansion is to be deemed 'excessive'? The answer depends on monetary policy, or rather the answer determines monetary policy. In the nineteenth century monetary policy was defined by the gold standard. A monetary expansion was excessive, if it outstripped the world supply of gold, if, that is, after the industrial demand for gold was met, what was left proved insufficient to provide the gold coin and gold reserves required by the monetary systems of the world.

When gold ran short, Bank rate went up, and deflation followed, not only in England, but throughout the gold-using world. Had the gold supply failed over a long period to keep pace with the demand for gold, a monetary contraction might have become necessary without any preceding expansion. But that did not occur. Even in periods such as 1815–49, and 1873–96, when prices in terms of gold were on balance falling, the alternation of monetary expansions and contractions prevailed. Gold provided an automatic indicator of the monetary position and a guide to credit policy. No such indicator or guide is available now. All the monetary systems adhering to the International Monetary Fund are ostensibly on a gold standard. That the gold parity of any of their money units is liable to be altered in case of a 'fundamental disequilibrium', and that the whole set of gold parities might, in certain eventualities, be changed in a uniform proportion, these are important modifications of the traditional gold standard. But what is of more immediate practical significance is the gold position of the United States, whose gold holding is so vast that the wealth-value of gold is effectively determined by that of the dollar, and gold affords no independent standard of value.

The International Monetary Fund accepts this situation and expresses parities indifferently in gold and in dollars, and throughout the world the American dollar is taken as the standard to which all money units are to be referred. But the dollar is no standard; its wealth-value varies according to American credit conditions, and American credit policy is not governed by any view as to what the wealth-value of its money unit ought to be. The pound sterling, like the dollar and all the other money units linked to the dollar, is adrift.

The most urgent need of the pound sterling is a monetary standard to form the basis of British credit policy. If measures were taken to stabilise the wealth-value of the American dollar, gold would likewise be stabilised, and parity with gold would supply an acceptable standard. Failing a stable dollar, credit policy could be directed to maintaining a stable pound.

A stable pound means a pound of unvarying wealth-value. But wealth-value measured by the reciprocal of an index number of prices does not quite meet the case. It is true that the value of the money unit in terms of any particular product is measured by the inverse of the price of the product. But the price of any product is affected by various conditions other than the value of money; by real cost and by transitory states of relative scarcity or abundance. An index number averages the prices of a selection (perhaps a wide selection) of commodities, but the special circumstances affecting particular commodities cannot be safely assumed to average out. Technological progress is always reducing real costs, so that the price level tends downwards independently of the value of the money unit, and this tendency is sure to be irregular and intermittent.

Real cost means in the last resort cost in terms of human effort, and stable money is best defined as that which maintains the money value of human effort unvarying. The money value of human effort depends of course on the kind of effort, but at the basis is the remuneration of the time given by a worker of no exceptional qualifications. In a given state of society the remuneration of higher grades, extending up to technicians, experts and administrators, is linked with the basic wage level by recognised relativities, conforming ultimately to a competitive system.

Stable money is best defined as that which is consistent with an unvarying basic wage level. If credit is so regulated that the flow of money just suffices to pay for the output corresponding to full employment at prices which remunerate enterprise with normal profits, stability is attained. Under the expression 'normal profits' is concealed a wide variety of profit margins, corresponding to all possible states of industry, ranging from prosperous expansion to hopeless decline. The transfer of labour from the declining industries to the expanding cannot be instantaneous. The time inevitably intervening is one of the sources of that minimum of unemployment of which a policy of full employment cannot expect to be rid. A characteristic of over-employment is that hardly any industry finds demand so poor that it has any labour to spare, and the prosperous industries are prevented by the shortage of labour from expanding. Stability requires that the demand for labour in the expanding industries should be sufficient to provide employment (not necessarily directly) for those displaced from the declining industries. It is for the labour market as a whole to sort them out. The sorting process applies in the first instance to the young recruits, but the mobility of labour is usually sufficient to lead to considerable transfers in the main body of workpeople.

It follows that a credit policy aiming at stable money will look primarily to the state of the labour market, or rather to the state of sales and of profits by which the demand for labour is governed. If the volume of orders increases beyond that corresponding to full employment, tighter credit is needed to prevent inflation starting; if the volume of orders falls off, a relaxation of credit may be needed to prevent unemployment.

Bankers are well placed to be early aware of these tendencies, and therefore to take early action. The weak point of the gold standard, as worked in the nineteenth century, was that early action was not taken; the effect of an undue expansion of credit on gold reserves was felt too late, and, by the time action was taken, a drastic application of dear money had become necessary. It was the heavy deflation by which the gold reserve position was restored that caused serious spells of depression and unemployment. Had early action been taken, and the flow of money been prevented from expanding beyond what the supply of gold would allow, deflation would never have been necessary, and the reserves would have been all the more effectively protected.

The same mechanism for regulating credit which was used to maintain the gold standard could be applied, without this defect, to maintaining the stability of the pound. And the reserve of gold and dollars would still play a part. A loss of reserves would be a sign of an adverse balance. But the monetary authorities would not be committed to imposing tight credit to correct it; they would have to diagnose the situation, and to decide whether the adverse balance was due to a credit expansion at home, or to a credit contraction or some other cause abroad. Only in the former case would tight credit be the right remedy; in the latter a depreciation of the money unit would be appropriate. So long as the wealth-value of gold is governed by that of a fluctuating dollar, a policy of stabilising the pound will require adjustments (possibly frequent) of gold parity and of the rate of exchange, as well as of Bank rate.

In my *Bretton Woods for Better or Worse* (pp. 99–105) I adduced grounds for thinking that variable rates of exchange need not be a very serious impediment to international trade. Traders bargaining to receive or pay foreign money in the course of their proceedings can eliminate the exchange risk by entering into a forward sale or purchase of an equivalent amount for their own money. Forward markets in foreign exchange are not everywhere to be found quoting reasonable rates. But so far as the market in pounds and dollars is concerned, an active forward market can be assumed.

In that work I argued that stability of wealth-value of a money unit employed in international trade is more important than stability of its foreign-exchange value.[1] Traders dealing in the great British commodity markets reckon their prices in pounds sterling. Their special knowledge relates to the conditions affecting the products they deal in, and they do not want their calculations to be upset by unpredictable fluctuations in the money they base them on.

The pound sterling is fated to be an international currency, because it is the money unit of a country which cannot live without a great volume of imports and exports. British wages express the money value of the costs of British

[1] *Bretton Woods for Better or Worse* (1946), pp. 105–7.

manufactured exports, which constitute a considerable fraction of the manufactured goods sold in international markets. An appreciable part of the materials dealt in in the British commodity markets are destined to be bought for the use of British manufacturers supplying export markets. Thus British wages, being, along with the world prices of materials, the essential factor in the prices of British exports, a stabilisation of the pound which would make wages substantially constant in terms of money would supply a firm monetary basis for the trade of the world.

Needless to say, a rigidly constant wage level is not to be expected. There are sure to be wage adjustments here and there, especially in the more prosperous industries, and, the resistance to wage reductions being what it is, these adjustments are likely on balance to amount to an increase. But in the absence of a monetary expansion the increase is likely to be slight and gradual. In the period from about 1850 to 1914 wages in Great Britain approximately doubled. That was only possible, consistently with an unvarying gold parity, because the world's gold supply expanded. But the average annual increase in the wage level was only about one per cent. A policy of stabilisation based on the wage level would prevent the monetary system from ever itself giving the ground for a rise in the wage level.

A stabilisation of the pound sterling by the instrumentality of credit, unless accompanied by a stabilisation of the American dollar, would necessitate a variable rate of exchange on the United States. That might entail resignation of Great Britain from the International Monetary Fund.

The variable rate, however, would not be asked for till sound finance and tight credit had led to a favourable balance of payments, an accumulation of reserves and an upward pressure in the market on the pound. Those conditions would open the way to free convertibility of the pound, an untrammelled convertibility such as it is usual at present to regard as beyond hope in the near future. A convertibility of sterling which might include a complete abandonment of exchange control, as well as of import restrictions, would be more liberal than the convertibility stipulated in the American Loan Agreement of December 1945 and would go far to reconcile American opinion to a variable rate of exchange.

Is this claiming too much? That an adverse balance is due to over-spending is a matter of arithmetic, hardly open to dispute. That overspending depends on the supply of money is self-evident. The supply of money is derived either from existing balances or from bank advances. Any superfluity in existing balances can be extinguished by prudent Government finance: adequate taxation, supplemented by loans calculated to draw on investible savings. Bank advances can be regulated by a wisely directed credit policy.

Credit policy is of prime importance because it operates on the vast mass of wealth constituting traders' stocks. By putting a check to active accumulation, it has the power not merely to stop over-spending, but, for a time, to turn active accumulation of stocks into a negative quantity, and so to make room for much immediate expenditure on armaments or on capital outlay, which would otherwise cause over-spending.

It is only after excess spending has been thus brought to an end that a long-range policy aiming at the stabilisation of money will come into view.

WELFARE, CAPITAL AND DEFENCE

Over-spending has been made possible by the existence of redundant money and by easy credit. But there is another side of the question. Spending is composed of consumption, capital formation and defence expenditure (other Government expenditure can be included under the two former heads), and policy has been pressing for the enlargement of each of these. Up to 1950 special resources were available to cover the over-spending which policy insisted on. Now the special resources have come to an end. For the moment import restrictions have provided for excess spending on consumption, capital outlay and defence, by forcing a decrease in stocks. Tight credit could dispense with the restriction of imports by making a lower level of stocks acceptable, and so discouraging active accumulation. But the reduction of stocks cannot go on for ever. Eventually the country must choose on what it is to retrench. Is it to impose austerity, and reduce consumption? Is it to let capital outlay decline, and suffer a disastrous setback to productivity and to competitive power? Swollen armament expenditure would require one or the other. If we could assume that armament expenditure will subside in a few years, a reduction in the acceptable level of stocks might suffice to provide the requisite resources. A prolonged period of tight credit would do no harm; its function would be to release productive power for armaments and for capital outlay by reducing stocks instead of by reducing consumption. Productive activity would continue undiminished, and full employment would be maintained.

But we cannot assume that armament expenditure will not continue unabated, after the margin of resources provided from stocks has been exhausted. If it does continue, there will be a conflict between consumption and capital outlay.

I have referred to capital outlay as an object of policy. But it would be difficult to specify just what the policy is. If there were no technological progress, the capital outlay would be confined to necessary renewals (paid for out of depreciation) and extensions corresponding to growth of population (the 'widening' of capital). But technological progress ever points the way to new labour-saving devices and to mechanism which enlarges the output of a given manpower (the 'deepening' of capital). It thereby makes possible an increased productivity and therefore a higher standard of living of a given population. In the conflict between capital outlay and consumption, capital outlay can claim to represent the future. 'In the long run we are all dead', but the future towards which capital outlay points is not distant; improved plant begins to yield fruit as soon as it comes into operation, and usually pays off its first cost in a moderate term of years.

On the other hand, we do not want to inflict privation in the present to gain increased affluence in the future, if a degree of affluence will in any case be attained such as to make people value any accession of wealth far less highly. Austerity was justifiable immediately after the war, because enforced accumulation was essential to set industry going, and nice calculations were not needed.

But to treat the conflict as one between welfare now and welfare in the future is to take too narrow a view of it. If industry is stinted of capital development, its competitive power in export markets will deteriorate. Its competitive power, it may be said, could then be restored by such devaluation of the pound as would equalise costs, and this devaluation would merely reflect the retarded progress in the standard of living already admitted. But competitive power is not maintained so easily. Technological progress is apt to affect particular industries unequally and discontinuously. A progressive industry depends mainly on its own resources in reinvested profits for its capital development. If it fails to keep pace with its competitors it gets into a vicious circle; because it is falling behind, its resources dwindle, and, for want of resources, it falls further behind.

When an important export industry thus drops out, the transfer of productive capacity into other industries may cause great economic loss, and if the effort to push this productive capacity into an alternative export business by a devaluation is carried too far, it may meet with failure in the same way as the devaluation of 1949.

It is not necessary to labour the argument. The conclusion that, if British industry were kept short of the capital resources needed for technological progress, the effect on its export trade would be ruinous would command general assent.

We have been assuming capital progress and armaments to be two separate questions. But they are in some respects inter-dependent. The defence expenditure in peace time is devoted to preparedness, that is, to providing the country with the means of meeting the first impact of war. After the first impact, its fighting power depends upon its war potential, upon an industry which can be adapted to a sustained production of all that the war effort requires. A high war potential demands a highly capitalised and mechanised industry adapted for mass production, which can only be built up by substantial and unremitting capital outlay in peace time.

So, even from the standpoint of defence, we cannot afford to let capital outlay fall off. We may go so far as to say that, in a world dominated by power politics, the contribution of capital development to the war potential claims priority over its contribution to welfare. The contribution to welfare is a fortunate by-product.

And defence expenditure itself cannot claim absolute priority over capital outlay. Preparedness is the more immediate need, but the war potential is the foundation of a sustained war effort, and therefore of power.

AUSTERITY

Since policy favours capital outlay and defence expenditure, and over-spending cannot continue indefinitely, it is consumption that must give way. The practical question then is how much austerity the public will stand.

The Soviet Union was confronted with this question in its early days. The industrialisation achieved by the successive five-year plans has been revealed as primarily a development of war potential. There a collectivist economic system places the whole 'surplus', composed of profit, rent and interest, at the disposal of a dictatorship. The dictators do not have to ask what degree of austerity the people will stand; they can impose whatever standard of living their policy of capital development and armaments permits and there is no room for either opposition or resistance.

With that system the democratic capitalist countries have to compete. There are two ways of imposing austerity: by rationing and by taxation.

Rationing is vexatious and requires an expensive administration. It involves a widespread misdirection of distribution in that the ration cannot take account of individual tastes and preferences.

And rationing, in any case, cannot cover the whole ground. It may be necessary in case of acute scarcity of a product which has to be made available to people of all grades of income, or to regulate the distribution of a product of which imports have to be restricted. But as an instrument of austerity it is clumsy and of only partial efficacy.

The policy of austerity during and after the war never relied exclusively on controls. It was always accompanied by measures of taxation on a scale which, when war expenditure abated, produced large surpluses to reinforce the country's capital resources.

Taxation imposes austerity on the taxpaper by curtailing the means of spending available to him. But it is subject to the drawback that it leaves him free to decide how to allocate the reduction in his resources between consumption and saving.

Fiscal policy has been designed in a spirit of equalitarianism. The wealthy can better dispense with their luxuries and superfluities than the poor with their comforts and necessaries. The main burden of taxation has been imposed on the larger incomes, and especially upon profits.

Direct taxation may be said to have been put on a peacetime basis in 1947. Income tax then began to be paid at the rate reduced from 10s. to 9s. by the budget of 1946, and after 31st December 1946 profits ceased to be subject to excess profits tax. If the revenue from excess profits tax (presumably already covered by tax reserves at the end of

1946) be excluded, the taxation of income from profits and interest has increased as follows (in £ millions):

TABLE XVII

	1947	1948	1949	1950	1951	1952
Income Tax	596	655	781	808	788	946
Surtax	60	76	85	87	95	97
Profits Tax	31	154	257	264	301	378
	687	885	1,123	1,159	1,184	1,421

The total of profits taxed had of course increased as the value of money fell, but in a much smaller proportion. The Excess Profits Levy of 1952 was an additional burden, but is now to cease.

A very significant occurrence was the increase in Surtax associated with the reduction of income tax in 1946. War-time taxation had so raised the two taxes together that the recipient of an income exceeding £20,000 a year only retained 6d. in the £ of the excess, and in 1946 this part of the surtax was raised by 1s., so that the reduction of income tax by that amount still left the surtax-payer with only 6d. in the £ of this part of his income.

On the other hand, the surtax-payer was allowed the benefit of the reduction of income tax by 6d. in 1953, so that he now retains 1s. in the £ of any excess of his income over £20,000. Not a very liberal allowance, but, so far as it goes, it tends to favour saving, and to alleviate the living on capital.

We have seen that in the year 1952 capital resources made a fairly good showing, and actually covered external investment as well as capital outlay at home. But the favourable result was due to the budget position, which provided a surplus (after adjustment) of £389 million and £120 million added to tax reserves. It will not outlast the weak budget of 1953, the deficiencies of which are already visible in the reliance of Government finance on bank credit.

Government finance is the root of the matter. Tight credit may for a time counteract its inflationary effect; it may do more, and so restrict active accumulation that redundant money is temporarily eliminated. But the effects of over-spending cannot be fended off for long.

But what can financial policy do? Loans which appeal to the long-term investor are not a solution. They are a direct drain on capital resources and are only recommended as a way of avoiding renewed inflation.

Unless we are to revert to the war-time system of austerity through rationing and other controls, austerity must be imposed through taxation, and the taxation must be so devised as to fall on consumption and not on saving. How are we to reconcile financial policy with the Welfare State?

Seemingly we are finding ourselves in the hard and treacherous path foreshadowed in my *Economic Rebirth* (p. 110), 'from conflict of aims to cross-purposes, from cross-purposes to dilemma, from dilemma to morass'.

A capitalist country can only draw on its surplus, composed of profits, rent and interest, on condition that the taxpayer is free to spend what is left to him as he chooses. If enough is left to him to provide an adequate fund of current saving, he is likely to take more for himself than a policy of austerity can afford to allow him. Equalitarian financial measures have gone too far, and current saving has been excessively reduced. Savings are also derived from the mass of salary-earners and wage-earners, but in the aggregate they are much less considerable and less variable than those derived from profits.

If taxation is to be the instrument of austerity, it must concentrate on the main body of consumers, and, in the incidence upon the profit-makers, must compromise with the need for maintaining savings.

It was this prospect that impelled me to write in 1946 (*Economic Rebirth*, p. 112), 'Will the profit-makers offer a direct challenge to the wage-earners, and claim that their own margin must be maintained even at the expense of the wage-earners' standard of living? Even if they or some of them think that that would be the right solution, surely it is not practical politics. Against them would be rallied both the forces of democracy and those of organised labour. Even the unwilling would have to bow to the inevitable.'

'Whether heroic measures will really be necessary', I added (p. 113), 'remains to be seen.' By heroic measures I meant collectivism—the complete nationalisation of profit-making. But 'if it is to come, it must be not merely as the exploit of a Socialist movement, but with the consent, even at the urgent demand, of all classes' (p. 119). In that event the co-operation of industrialists, merchants and financiers would be forthcoming.

Substantially 'heroic measures' then would mean making the State the sole shareholder or the residuary sleeping partner of all industrial and commercial concerns (as it is of the Bank of England, and was recently of the steel companies). Presumably collectivism initiated in the traditional English spirit of compromise would provide compensation for the former shareholders. The result would not be very different in principle from the limitation of dividends informally imposed by the Socialist Government, but would be more far-reaching in that it would apply to the profits of partnerships as well as of companies, and that the annuities which would replace the dividends would be permanently fixed and would presumably be less than the dividends (the steel shareholders who retained the Government securities by which they were compensated suffered a loss of income).

Heroic measures of this kind do not seem to be any nearer now than they were seven years ago. But the dilemma which led me to speculate on them then was and still remains a real one. A friendly critic commented at the time that a collectivist system would after all turn out to be no solution, because the incentives to enterprise would be disastrously weakened. That is the classical argument against collectivism, deriving ultimately from Adam

Smith's 'invisible hand', and I am not prepared to dispute it. But it might not be accepted as decisive if the situation I imagined in 1946 became imminent.

All this is still a remote speculation. What is likely to be an urgent problem in the near future is the immediate need for a fiscal policy and a credit policy which will put an end to excess spending, and to the inflation and adverse balance of payments which it causes. That once accomplished, the state of current savings and capital enterprise can be considered in the light of the world political situation and the needs of defence.

INDEX

Acceptable level of stocks, 85, 86–92, 108, 137
Acceptance credits, 100
Accommodating payments, 83
Active accumulation of stocks, 85–8, 107–8, 124–5, 136
Advances, Bank, *see* Bank
Adverse balance of payments
  caused by excess spending, 6, 14, 39, 41, 72, 85, 120, 128–129, 136, 144
  a capital resource, 6, 58, 87
  Statistics of, 6, 28–9, 35, 48–9, 57, 94–7
  with Dollar Area, 6–7, 28–9, 38, 44, 48–9, 96–7, 108, 113
  replenishes stocks, 14, 58, 87
  and American aid, 25, 28–9, 39
  and convertibility, 25, 29
  and import restrictions, 25–7, 33–5, 39–40
  and rate of exchange, 31–3, 108, 113
  and credit policy, 40–1, 59, 79, 85, 108
  checked by dear money, 41, 108
  and terms of trade, 46, 48, 59
  and competition, 72, 120
  met by Special Resources, 83, 94, 97
  and external investment, 94–8
  and inflation, 122, 128–9, 144
Agreements, Payments, 23, 97
Allocation of materials, 3, 12, 39
Allowances, Voluntary, 14
American (*see also* United States)
  loan, 1, 5–7, 23, 25, 28–9, 42, 50, 87, 99
  agreement of 6 Dec. 1945, 7, 11, 22, 136

prices, 7, 20–1, 30, 36–7, 43–4, 68, 114, 127
wages, 7, 31, 37, 44, 47, 65, 68–70, 120
exportable surpluses, 19
manufactures, 19–21, 24, 69–71, 97–8, 119–20
price control, 19–21, 30, 36
stocks (inventories), 19–21, 30, 36
support of bond market, 20–1, 38
aid (Marshall Aid or E.R.P.), 24, 25, 28–9, 33, 39, 42, 49, 87, 94
unemployment, 30, 68, 113
index of production, 30-1, 38, 70
imports, 36, 38
gold reserve, 38, 131
credit policy, 68–9
productivity, 69–71
mass production, 71, 119–20
tariff, 119–20
individuality products, 120
Anglo-American Agreement of 6 Dec. 1945, 7, 11, 22, 136
Anglo-Iranian Oil Co., 50
Annuities, 14, 112, 143
Appreciation of stocks, 53–5, 60, 62–3
  Taxation of, 53–4, 58, 60–1
Armaments (*see also* Defence), 48, 50, 53, 60–1, 109, 136–7, 139–40
Arrears of
  capital outlay, 5, 16, 103
  expenditure, 6, 16–17, 24, 39–40, 42
  exports, 35
  maintenance, 3, 12, 16

Austerity
  Wartime, 3, 142
  and rationing, 3, 123, 140, 142
  and controls, 17, 19, 39, 142
  and exports, 17, 123
  and imports, 39–40, 123
  and saving, 137, 142
  Post-war, 138, 140
  and excess spending, 138–9
  and taxation, 140–3

Balance of Payments
  Adverse, *see* Adverse Balance of Payments
  Dollar
    British, 6–7, 28–9, 44, 48, 96–7, 108, 117
    of overseas Sterling Area, 28, 38, 49, 96–7, 102, 113
  Favourable, 29, 58, 62, 93, 108, 117, 120, 122, 135
  and rates of exchange, 31–2, 108, 113
  and stocks, 57–8, 87–8
  and credit policy, 59, 79, 135
  and invisibles, 93
  over-all, 96–7, 108, 117
Bank
  advances
    to Government, 13, 15, 81, 104, 106, 121, 123, 141
    Interest on, 41, 74–5, 76–80, 102–3
    and excess spending, 41, 73, 77, 85, 103, 136
    for capital outlay, 41, 75–6 102–3
    generate money, 41, 73, 136
    amount of, 42, 67, 80, 91, 104, 121
    Restriction of, 59, 79–80, 83
    Reduction of 67
    supersede bills, 67
  deposits, 13, 15, 41, 67, 73, 105, 121
  notes, 13, 73
  assets, 15, 41, 73, 81, 91, 104
  of England, 27, 73–5, 81, 118, 143
  rate
    and post-war inflation, 41
    Rise of, in 1951–2, 59, 79, 83, 87
    Minimum, 59
    and discount market, 74
    and interest on bank advances, 74
    and Treasury bills, 74–5
    and industrial activity, 77, 124
    Flexible, 80, 82–3, 120, 125
    Reduction of, in 1953, 82, 120
    and Government securities, 120, 124–5
    and active accumulation, 124
    and gold standard, 130
  reserves, 73
Bankers, Early action by, 133
Banks, the source of money, 13, 41, 73, 104, 136
Barter, 129
Basic wage level, 132, 135
Beveridge, Lord, 126
Bills
  Treasury, 13, 15, 73–5, 81, 104, 106
  of exchange, 74, 100
Borrowing (*see also* Bank advances, Government securities, Treasury bills)
  for capital outlay, 41, 75–6, 102
  by investment market, 41, 102
  diminished by tax reserves, 53
  and Bank rate, 75
  by consumers, 75
  for replenishment of stocks, 76
  for purchase of goods, 76–7
  for expenses of production, 78
  by speculators, 102
  for long-term assets, 103
Breakdown, Monetary, 7, 12, 19, 25, 129–30
Bretton Woods, 43
Bretton Woods for Better or Worse, 134
British
  impoverishment, 1, 12
  mercantile profits, 2

external investments, 2, 12, 29, 94, 98, 99–102, 103–4, 141
shipping, 2
exporting power, 2, 5, 71–2
exports, 2, 7, 9, 28, 46, 65, 71–72, 99–100, 119, 134–5
  of manufactures, 46, 71, 98, 116
imports, 2, 9, 26, 47, 50, 59, 99
  of food, 2, 26
  of materials, 2, 26, 47, 48
costs, 4, 31, 37, 44, 47, 66, 72, 116, 118–19, 127, 135, 138
wages
  index, 4, 15, 16, 44, 47, 60, 111–12
  at end of war, 15
  Rise of, 15, 60, 65, 68, 111–114, 118
  and American, 31, 37, 44, 65, 69–70
  and devaluation, 31, 37, 44, 65–6, 68
  and export costs, 31, 44, 127–8, 135
capital outlay, 5–6, 54–7, 137–139, 141–2
dollar balance, 6–7, 28–9, 44, 48, 96–7, 108, 117
reserves, 9, 27, 117, 120, 129, 135
  Losses and gains of, 7, 23, 29–30, 33–4, 37, 48–9, 59, 95, 120
Exchange control, 8–12, 19, 24, 30–1, 101, 104, 109, 136
prices, 14–15, 18, 44, 60, 65, 68
dollar exports and imports, 34–6
defence expenditure, 50, 61
credit system, 73–5
mercantile community, 99
Budget
  of 1946, 6, 51–2
  deficit, 6, 15, 80–2, 89, 104
  American, 38
  of 1951, 51, 53, 60
  surplus, 53, 61, 81, 87, 121, 140, 141
  of 1952, 61, 121

  of 1953, 81, 121, 141
  weakness, 123, 141
Bulk purchasing, 17, 45

Call loans, 74
Canadian loan, 1, 5–6, 23, 28–9, 42, 50, 87, 99
Capital
  formation, 3–5, 39, 54–7, 62, 83, 85–6, 122, 136
  equipment, 3, 5, 32, 84, 105
  depreciation, 3–5, 21, 57, 82, 112, 137
  Deterioration of, 3
  outlay
    British, 5–6, 54–7, 137–9, 141–2
    arrears of, 5, 16, 103
    and excess spending, 6, 13, 39–41, 136
    Licensing of, 12, 17
    Excess, 58, 95
    by Government, 60–2, 81–2, 84, 121, 123
    and credit policy, 83–4
    and controls, 105
    policy, 84, 137, 139–40
  extensions, 5, 77, 102, 105, 107, 124, 137
  Working (*see also* Stocks), 5, 55, 63, 84
  movements, 8, 11, 19, 39n., 101
  resources (*see also* Saving)
    Statistics of, 6, 57, 93, 95–6, 141
    and capital outlay, 6, 58, 93, 125
    provided by Government, 12, 53, 58, 61–2, 88, 107, 122–3, 140–2
    and external investment, 12, 96, 141
    and austerity, 136–41
Capital
  issues, 12, 104n.
  Raising of, 12, 40, 76, 82, 106–107, 124–5
  Taxes on, 53, 57
  Fixed, 54
  Yield of, 82, 103

Capital (*cont.*)
  accumulation and austerity, 84, 138, 142
  Living on, 84, 141
  Widening and deepening, of 137
  development and competitive power, 138–9
Capitalist country, 140, 142
Cheap money, 79, 108, 120
Civilian spending, 14–15
Clearing, 73
Clothing, Rationing of, 17
Coal, 17, 27
Coin, Gold, 130
Collectivist system, 139, 143
Colonies, Sterling held in, 109–110
Commodity markets, 116, 134–5
Company reserves, 5, 54, 102, 105, 107, 112
Comparative costs, 117
Competition
  American, 31, 45, 71, 97, 113, 119–20
  of manufacturers, 46
  German and Japanese, 71, 119
  for labour, 119, 128
  of capital outlay with Government flotations, 124–5
Competitive power, 45, 137–8
Competitive system, 132
Conditional aid, 94
Congestion of orders, 18–19, 21, 25, 30, 32, 37, 85, 107, 109, 125
Congress, United States, 33
Conservative Government, 59
Consols, 106
Construction, Licensing of, 12, 17
Consumers, Borrowing by, 75
Consumers' preferences, 72, 140
Consumption
  and shop shortages, 5
  and adverse balance, 6, 39
  and imports, 6, 38–40, 66
  and spending, 13, 39, 83–4, 86
  and controls, 14
  of stock-held products, 39
  and saving, 40, 83, 137, 140, 142
  and prices, 66
  and taxation, 142
Control
  Exchange, 8–12, 19, 24, 30–1, 100, 101, 104, 109, 136
  of capital issues, 12, 104n.
  of capital outlay, 12, 17, 125
  Price, 14, 15, 18, 19–21, 40, 87, 127–8
  of man-power, 15
  of wages, 15, 39, 118
  of rents, 112
Controls, 2–3, 12, 14, 29, 39–40, 66, 103, 125
  Evasion of, 9, 12, 101
  Relaxation of, 20, 36, 50, 87, 123, 125
Convenience in holding of stocks, 76–7
Conventional bank interest, 74, 79
Convertibility, 7, 11–12, 19, 21, 23–5, 29, 135
Cost of living, 15
Costs
  and wages, 4, 15, 47, 108
  Exporters' 9, 31, 44–7, 66, 72, 116, 118, 119, 127, 135
  Manufacturers', 46, 63, 72
  and undervaluation, 65, 118
  Comparative, 117
  Real, 132
Cotton, 64
Creation of money by banks, 13, 41, 73–5, 78, 81, 89, 93, 106
Credit
  Creation of, 13, 41, 81
  contraction, 37, 68–9, 92, 134
  Easy, 38, 40
  Tight, 41, 85, 87–8, 90, 102, 107–8, 133–7
  policy, 59, 80–5, 91, 102, 108, 131, 133, 136, 144
  regulation, 59, 82, 85, 117, 133
  Concerted restriction of, 59, 79–80, 83
  Relaxation of, 82, 90–1, 128, 133

Instability of, 82, 86
Commercial, 100
to importers, 100
Credits, Acceptance, 100
Cripps, Sir Stafford, 123
Crises, 123
Crisis, Fuel, 7, 27
Currency
Hard, 8–12, 22, 26n., 30
International, 8–9, 25, 43, 131, 134
Soft, 9–11, 21–2, 26n., 30, 31
Supply of, 73
Current transactions, 11, 22

Damage, War, 3, 5, 6, 57
Dealers
Wholesale and retail, 89
in investment market, 41, 102, 106
Dear money, 41, 68, 80, 90–2, 102, 108, 124
Death duties, 57
Declining industries, 132–3
Deepening of capital, 137
Defence Aid, 58, 61
Defence expenditure (*see also* Armaments), 50, 61, 84, 88, 89, 139, 144
Deficit, Budget, 6, 15, 80–2, 89, 104
Deflation, 37, 43–4, 130, 133
Delays in delivery, 24, 30, 44, 119
Demand
and prices, 13, 18, 32, 36, 45, 89–90, 113
for labour, 15, 32, 65, 89–90, 119, 125, 127, 133
and controls, 17, 32
and price control, 18–19, 40
for dollars, 24–5
for imports, 32, 66
for materials, 36, 46, 48, 113
Decline of, 36, 113, 124, 130
Expansion of, 45, 89, 124
for finished products, 46
engendered by import of capital, 98
for primary products, 113, 115
for investible funds, 104, 124–125
for gold, 130

Demobilisation, 3
Democracy, 143
Depreciation
of capital, 3–5, 21, 57, 82, 112, 137
of money unit, 31–3, 43, 110, 122–3, 128, 134
Depression, 16, 37, 44, 133
Devaluation
Conditions leading to, 30–1, 33, 36–8
and export costs, 31–2, 45–7, 65–6, 108, 116
and imports, 31, 32, 45, 47, 66–7
and wages, 31, 37, 46–7, 60, 65–6, 68–9, 111, 113, 118–19
and prices, 32, 45–7, 60, 65, 67–9, 109, 116, 123
and American pressure, 33
and speculation against sterling, 33–4, 35, 36
decided on in August 1949, 34
agreed to by I.M.F., 34, 43–4, 114
and competitive power, 45, 98, 119–20
and terms of trade, 45–7, 59, 123
abroad, 45, 47, 67
and inflation, 69, 109, 111–12, 118
and sterling balances, 110, 111
involves revaluation payments, 110
intensifies over-employment, 44–5, 98, 127
Dictators, 139
Direct investments, 102
Direct taxation, 140
Discount market, 74
Discount on sterling, 30–1, 45
Disinvestment, 1, 3
Dislocation caused by inflation, 111, 112, 118, 128
Displaced labour, 132–3
Disposable profits, 54, 62–4
Distrust of money, 18, 29–30, 124, 129–30
Diversification of industry, 120
Dividends, 54, 103, 143

Division of Labour, International
Dollar
  balance
    British, 6–7, 28–9, 44, 96–7, 108, 117
    of Sterling Area, 6–7, 28, 38, 49, 96–7, 102, 112
  Area
    Formation of, 10–11
    Exports to, 22, 34–6, 49–50
    Imports from, 34–6, 49–50, 67, 98
  rate of exchange, 24, 33, 36, 43, 69, 113, 134
  Purchasing power of, 24
  Pre-eminence of, 24, 131
  Instability of, 43, 113–14, 131
  as world standard, 43, 131
  reserves, *see* Reserves
Dollars
  as hard currency, 8, 21–2, 30
  Demand for, 24–5

Early action by bankers, 133
Easy credit, 38, 40, 90
Economic Destiny, 41n.
Economic Rebirth, 41n., 111, 142–3
Economic rent, 46
Efficiency of labour, 69
Employment Act, U.S., 68
Employment (*see also* Full employment, Over-employment, Unemployment)
  Under-, 13, 26, 31, 39, 46, 90
  Decline of, 68, 85, 90, 125, 130
Endowments, 112
English credit system, 73–5
Enterprise, 143–4
Equalitarianism, 140, 142
Equipment, Capital, 3, 5, 32, 84, 105
Essential imports, 2, 5, 72
European Economic Cooperation Committee, 23
European Payments Union, 50, 95–6, 108
European Recovery Programme, *see* Marshall Aid
Evasion of controls, 9, 12, 101

Excess profits
  tax, 6, 51–2, 57, 140
  levy, 61, 121, 141
Excess spending
  by Government, 6, 13, 15, 92
  includes capital outlay, 6, 13, 39–41, 136
  means spending in excess of income and therefore of production, 13–14
  causes inflation, 13, 83, 144
  is met from stocks, 13–14, 83, 88, 92, 137
  and imports, 13–14, 40, 83, 137
  and adverse balance, 39, 41, 72, 85, 108, 120, 136, 144
  and supply of money, 39–41 77, 83, 92, 103, 106, 136
  and capital resources, 53, 58, 83
  on valuable assets, 84
  includes active accumulation of stocks, 85–6, 136–7
  and exports, 98
  and overseas sterling, 109
  and austerity, 139
Exchange (*see also* Foreign exchange market, Rate of exchange)
  control, 8–12, 19, 24, 30–1, 100, 101, 104, 109, 136
  Equalisation Account, 27, 96, 117
  Bills of, 74, 100
  stability, 114–15
  Forward market in, 116, 134
Expanding industries, 132–3, 138
Export
  markets, 2–3, 31, 45, 87
  drive, 3, 17, 28, 45, 71, 87–8, 123
  trade, 71, 119
Exportable goods, 17, 87, 127
Exporters overloaded with orders, 21, 25, 30
Exporters'
  costs, 9, 31, 44–7, 66, 72, 116, 118, 119, 127, 135
  profits, 32, 46–7

Exporting power, 2, 31, 71–2, 98
Exports
  Volume of, 2, 28, 32, 45, 71
  British, 2, 7, 9, 28, 46, 65, 71–72, 99–100, 134–5
    of manufactures, 71, 98, 116
  payment for, 9, 11
  Proceeds of, 9, 11, 32, 45, 93, 98, 116, 123
  Invisible, 22, 93
  to Dollar Area, 22, 34–6, 49–50
  Prices of, 31–2, 45, 47, 64, 128
  Extension of, 32, 45, 98, 128
Extensions, Capital, 5, 77, 102, 105, 107, 124, 137
External
  disinvestment, 1
  investment, 2, 8, 12, 19, 93–6, 98–105, 141
  payments, 8–11
  resources, 9, 12, 100
Externally held sterling, *see* Sterling balances

Fashion, 71
Favourable balance of payments, 29, 58, 62, 93, 108, 117, 120, 122, 135,
Final outlay, 54
Finance, Government, 6, 13, 15, 108, 128, 140, 142
Five-year Plans, 139
Fixed capital formation, 54
Flexible Bank rate, 80, 82–3, 120, 125
Flight of capital, 19, 39n.
Floating pound, 117
Flotations, 40, 76, 81–2, 106, 107, 124
Flow of money, 16, 18, 67–8, 132
Food
  Imported, 2, 26
  subsidies, 15, 61, 123
  Rationing of, 17, 39
Forced loan, 41, 107
Foreign
  assets, 9, 12, 100
  exchange market, 9, 118, 135
    Forward, 116, 134
  trade products, 127

Formation of capital, 3–5, 39, 54–7, 62, 83, 85–6, 122, 136
Forward
  purchase or sale, 63, 116, 134
  market in foreign exchange, 116, 134
Free convertibility, 135
French franc, 115, 124
Fuel crisis of 1947, 7, 27
Full employment
  in Great Britain in 1946, 16
  in United States in 1946, 20
  in 1949, 32
  and the wage level, 65, 132–3
  Policy of, 68, 90, 125–7, 132–3, 137
  inconsistent with increase in output, 89
  causes competition for labour, 119
  and minimum unemployment, 125–7, 132
  attainable, 130
  meaning of, 126–7, 130
Funded stock, 42, 81, 106, 125
Fundamental disequilibrium, 43–4, 114, 118, 131
Furniture, Rationing of, 17

German competition, 71, 119
  monetary reform, 129
Gold
  reserves, 7, 38, 131, 133
  Purchase of, 29, 97
  Loan, South African, 29
  standard, 31, 130–1, 133
  Value of, 38, 131
  and dollar, 38, 43, 131
  guarantee, 110
  parity, 114–15, 118, 131, 134–135
  coin, 130
  Supply of, 130, 133, 135
  Industrial demand for, 130
  Shortage of, 130
Government
  trading, 2
  finance, 6, 13, 15, 108, 128, 140, 142
  borrowing, 13, 106, 121, 123–125, 142

Government (*cont.*)
  from banks, 13, 15, 104, 106, 121, 123, 141
  spending, 13, 15, 86, 89–91, 104–5, 136
  securities, 15, 16, 20–1, 38, 42, 73, 104–8, 120
  and Bank rate, 120, 124–5
  Conservative, 59
  Socialist, 59, 60
  Capital outlay of, 60–2, 81–2, 84, 121, 123
  flotations, 81–2, 106–8, 124
Great Britain, *see* British
Growth
  of population, 5, 137
  of capital, 5, 137–9
  of stocks, 85

Hard currency, 8–12, 22, 26n., 30
Harrod, R. F., 99, 101
Hedging, 63, 116, 134
Heroic measures, 143
Home market, 26, 31
Hours, Working, 111–12
Housing, 12, 40, 60
Human effort, 132

Import restrictions
  in 1946, 5
  by licensing, 8, 11, 17
  and exchange control, 11, 19, 102, 136
  Wartime, 14
  part of austerity, 19, 39, 123, 140
  abroad, 25
  in the Sterling Area, 25, 27
  Complications of, 26
  at the time of devaluation, 32–34, 37–9, 50, 58
  and consumption, 38–40, 66
  and stocks, 38, 87–8, 137
  and unemployment, 26–7, 39
  an emergency remedy for an adverse balance, 25–6, 33–4, 39–40, 123, 129
  and liberalisation policy, 50, 120
  in 1951–2, 58–9, 87, 93, 120
  and rationing, 140

Importable goods, 127
Importers, Credit to, 100
Imports
  British, 2, 9, 26, 47, 50, 59, 99
  of food, 2, 26
  of materials, 2, 17, 26, 47, 48
  Indispensable, 2, 5, 72
  Permitted, 8, 66
  Licensing of, 8, 11, 17
  and stocks, 14, 38–9, 88, 107, 128
  Volume of, 19, 50, 59
  Invisible, 19, 108
  Prices of, 31, 32, 45, 66–7
  from Dollar Area, 34–6, 49–50, 67, 98
  Non-essential, 39, 66
Impoverishment, 1, 12
Improvements, 16, 40, 102, 105, 138
Incentives, 143
Income
  National, 20, 36, 66
    and production, 13–14
  tax, 51–2, 61, 121, 140–1
Incomes, Transfer, 14
Indispensable imports, 2, 5, 72
Individual preferences and rationing, 140
Individuality products, 120
Industrialisation, 72, 139
Inflation
  Wartime, 13–14, 41, 111
  and controls, 14, 17–18
  and redundant money, 17–18, 41–2, 92, 104, 107–8, 128
  in United States, 20–1, 24, 36–37, 43, 87
  and Government finance, 41–42, 81, 89–92, 104–8, 124–5, 142
  Relapse into, 81, 89, 93, 104, 121–2
  and excess spending, 83, 122, 128–30, 142
  and deficit, 89
  and maturities, 107
  in oversea Sterling Area, 111
  Dislocation caused by, 111, 112, 118, 128

from within and from outside, 122
and yield of securities, 124
Suppressed, 128
and over-employment, 128–9
Initial allowances of depreciation, 52, 60–1, 121
Innovations, 71–2
Insecurities of capital, 101
Instability of credit, 82, 86
Instrumental capital, 54
Insurance
  benefits, 14, 112
  National, 61, 112, 127
  Life, 112
Interest, *see* Long-term rate of interest, Short-term rate of interest
Intermediate products, 78
International
  trade, 2, 134
  markets, 8, 46, 120, 135
  currency, 8–9, 25, 43, 131, 134
  Monetary Fund, 29, 34, 43, 96, 109–10, 114–15, 118, 131, 135
  prices, 31, 46, 48
  Bank, 109–10
  division of labour, 120
Inventories, 19
Investment
  External, 2, 8, 12, 19, 93–6, 98–105, 141
  in Sterling Area, 12, 29, 94, 98–9, 101–2
  market, 40–1, 42, 75, 81, 102–108, 124
  and saving, 40, 75, 84, 103, 105
  Long-term, 81, 102–3, 123–5
  Medium-term, 103
  and wealth-value of money, 124
Investments, Direct, 102
Investors, 42, 75, 81, 102–3
Invisible exports and imports, 19, 22, 93, 108
"Invisible hand", 144
Irregular markets in sterling, 30–31, 45, 101

Japanese competition, 71, 119

Keynes, 7, 84, 103, 115
Korean War, 36, 48, 50, 109

Labour
  Demand for, 15, 32, 65, 89–90, 119, 125, 127, 133
  Organised, 15, 47, 143
  Efficiency of, 69
  -saving mechanism, 107, 124, 137
  International division of, 120
  Scarcity of, 124, 133
  Transfers of, 132–3
  Displaced, 132–3
Lag of wages behind prices, 63, 127–8
Latin America, 10
Learned societies, 112
Lend-lease, 5, 23
Liberalisation of trade, 50, 59, 66, 87, 123
Licensing
  of imports, 8, 11, 17
  of capital outlay, 12, 17
Life insurance, 112
Limitation of dividends, 143
Liquidation of working capital, 63
Liquidity, 73
Living
  Cost of, 15
  on capital, 84, 141
  Standard of, 112, 137–9, 143
Loan
  American, 1, 5–7, 23, 25, 28–9, 42, 50, 87, 99
  Canadian, 1, 5–6, 23, 28–9, 42, 50, 87, 99
  South African gold, 29
  Forced, 41, 107
Loans
  to Local Authorities, 60
  to extinguish redundant money, 105–8, 117, 136
Long-term
  rate of interest, 79, 103–4, 124–5
  investment, 81, 102–3, 123–5
  securities, 81, 105
Low wages, 128
Luxuries, 140

Manpower, 1, 3, 15
Manufactures
  Post-war shortage of, 3, 24
  American, 19–21, 24, 69–71,
    97–8, 119–20
  British exports of, 46, 71, 98,
    116
  Prices of, 46, 63
  Production of, 70
Market
  Home, 26, 31
  Investment, 40–2, 75, 81, 102–
    108, 124
  Labour, 133
Marketable securities, 16, 103
Markets
  Export, 2–3, 31, 45, 87
  International, 8, 46, 120, 135
  Irregular, in sterling, 30–1, 45,
    101
Marshall Aid, 23–5, 28–9, 33, 39,
  42, 49, 87, 94
Mass production, 71, 119–20,
  139
Materials
  British imports of, 2, 26, 48,
    64
  Allocation of, 3, 12, 39
  Imported, 17, 47
  Prices of, 48, 64, 109
  Stocks of, 76, 78
Maturities, 16, 106–7
Meade, Professor James, 83
Means of payment, 8, 13
Mechanisation, 69, 71, 107, 124,
  137
Medium-term investments, 105
Mercantile profits, 2
Minimum stocks, 5, 76–7, 85,
  91–2
Monetary
  breakdown, 7, 12, 19, 25, 129–
    130
  weakness, 12, 44
  policy, 42, 73, 75, 80, 83, 98,
    120, 130
  contraction, 44, 68, 107, 118,
    130–1
  expansion, 65, 68, 109, 118,
    122, 130–1, 133–4
  reform, German, 129

  standard, 130–6
  reserves, *see* Reserves
Money (*see also* Currency, Re-
    dundant Money)
  Creation of, 13, 41, 73–5, 78,
    81, 89, 93, 106
  Flow of, 16, 18, 67–8, 132
  Stagnation of, 16, 67
  Distrust of, 18, 29–30, 124,
    129–30
  Depreciation of, 31–3, 43, 110,
    122–3, 128, 134
  Supply of, 41, 68, 77, 83, 92,
    104, 107–8, 136
  Dear, 41, 68, 80, 90–2, 102,
    108, 124
  Cheap, 79, 108, 120
  Wealth-value of, 124, 134
Movable plant, 54
Multilateral settlements, 98

National
  income, 13–14, 20, 36, 66
  debt, 14, 38
  Insurance, 61, 112, 127
Natural resources, 2, 69
Necessaries, 140
Non-essential imports, 39, 66
Normal
  stocks, 83, 88
  unemployment, 127
  profits, 132
Note issue, 81

Obsolescence, 5
Official rates of exchange, 8, 24,
  30–1, 33
Orders to producers
  for replenishment of stocks,
    14, 77–8, 80, 85–6, 89–90
  for imported goods, 14, 79,
    107, 123
  by consumers or users, 14
  Congestion of, 18–19, 21, 25,
    30, 32, 37, 85, 107, 109, 125
  Unfilled, 37, 77, 85, 90
  and pricing, 46, 63
  Diminution of, 77–8, 85, 90,
    107
  Financing of, 78, 80
  and employment, 133

United States (*see also* Ame
  and Dollar Area 10–11
  Inflation, in 20–1, 24, 36–
   87
  Congress, 33
  National income of, 36
  Recession in, 44, 68, 11
  Unemployment in, 68
  Natural resources of, 69
  Speculation in, 103
  tariff, 119–20
Unjust steward, 110
Unrationed goods, 17, 9:
  129
Upkeep of property, 12, 1
Up-valuation of the poun
  120
Urge to spend, 16–18, 39

Valid rate of exchange, 3:
Value of gold, 38, 131
Vicious circle, 18, 32,
  118, 138
Volume of
  exports, 2, 28, 32, 45,
  imports, 19, 50, 59
Voluntary allowances, 14

Wage
  index, 4, 15, 16, 44,
   111
  level
   and inflation, 112
   Basic, 132, 135
  demands, 46, 89
  anomalies, 118
Wage-earners' savings, 1
Wages
  and costs, 4, 15, 31,
   108, 127–8, 135

O.E.E.C., 50, 59
Organised labour, 15, 47, 143
Overdrafts, 74–5
Over-employment
  and demand for labour, 15, 32, 65, 128
  caused by price control, 21, 127
  caused by excess spending, 24, 128–9
  caused by redundant money, 24, 127
  and fear of unemployment, 27, 37, 119, 125
  an impediment to export trade, 31–2, 44–5, 47, 98
  caused by undervaluation of the pound, 37, 118, 127–8
  and congestion of orders, 78, 109, 125
  an impediment to capital outlay, 105
  statistical test of, 126–7
  and inflation, 128–30

Pakistan, 67
Parity Gold, 114–15, 118, 131, 134–5
Payment
  for exports and imports, 9, 11
  Means of, 8, 13
Payments Agreements, 23, 97
Pension funds, 112
Pensions, 14, 112
Permitted imports, 8, 66
Persian oil, 50
Philanthropic donations, 14
Poincaré, 124
Points, Rationing by, 17
Political influences, 26, 37, 42, 139, 143, 144
Population, 2, 5, 137
Postponement
  of outlay, 5, 16, 42
  of renewals, 5, 16, 92
  of upkeep, 16, 92
Post-war credits, 51
Pound
  Weakness of, 12, 44
  Distrust of, 25, 29–30, 33, 124

Wealth-value of, 110–11, 124, 132
Under-valuation of, 37, 113–114, 118–19, 122, 127–8
Up-valuation of, 114–20
Floating, 117
Stabilisation of, 131, 133–6
Power politics, 139
Premium on early delivery, 89
Preparedness, 139
Price control, 14–15, 18–21, 40, 87, 127–8
Price reductions, 46, 90, 130
Price variation clause, 130
Prices
  Rise of, 3, 13, 18, 63, 89–90, 122, 128
  American, 7, 20–1, 30, 36–7, 43–4, 68, 113–14, 127
  and demand, 13, 18, 32, 36, 45, 66, 89–90, 113
  British, 14–15, 18, 44, 60, 65, 68
  of exports, 31–2, 45, 47, 64, 128
  of imports, 31–2, 45, 66–7
  of primary products, 36, 46, 109, 113, 115–16
  of manufactures, 46, 64
  of materials, 46–7, 64
  World, 46
  and profits, 46–7, 62–6, 132
  and wages, 63, 127–8
Primary products (*see also* Food, Materials), 36, 46, 109, 113, 115–16
Priority, 14
Production, 3, 5, 13
Productive capacity, 13, 30. 32, 45, 90, 98, 107, 124
Productivity, 69–71, 137
Profit margin, 46, 63, 132
Profits (*see also* Excess profits)
  Mercantile, 2
  on external investments, 2, 99, 102
  Reinvested (Undistributed) 21, 40–1, 53–4, 82, 102–3, 105
  High, 46–7, 102, 127
  tax, 51–2, 61
  Disposable, 54, 62–4

Sterling (*see also*
　an internationa
　　25, 134
　Speculation ag
　　101
　Irregular mark
　　101
　Discount on, 3
Stock-held good
Stockjobbers, 10
Stocks of goods
　and capital for
　　83–6
　Minimum, 5,
　and excess s
　　83, 88, 92, 1
　and imports,
　　83, 87–8, 10
　Replenishmen
　　58, 76, 80,
　and sales, 20,
　Strategic, 48,
　Appreciation
　　63
　Statistics of, 5
　Wholesale and
　held with bo
　　76, 85, 87,
　Manufacturer
　of materials,
　Reduction of,
　Normal, 83, 8
　Acceptable, 8:
　Long-range g
　Active accum
　　107–8, 124–
　Shortage of,
　of foreign tr
　　transit, 99–
Subsidies
　Food, 15, 61,
　Export, 119
Superfluities, 14
Surplus
　war stores, 6,
　Budget, 53,
　　140, 141
　National, 139
Surtax, 51, 141

Tariff, United